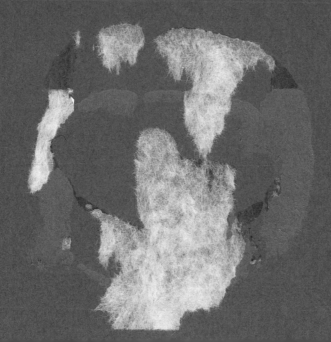

VALUES in an AGE OF CONFRONTATION

STUDIES OF THE PERSON

edited by

Carl R. Rogers

William R. Coulson

A Symposium
Sponsored by
The Religion in Education Foundation

VALUES IN AN AGE OF CONFRONTATION

Jeremiah W. Canning, editor

CHARLES E. MERRILL PUBLISHING COMPANY

A Bell & Howell Company   Columbus, Ohio

Copyright © 1970 by *Charles E. Merrill Publishing Company*, Columbus, Ohio. All rights reserved. No part of this book may be reproduced in any form, electronic or mechanical, including photocopy, recording, or any information storage and retrieval system, without permission in writing from the publisher.

Standard Book Number: 675-09349-X

Library of Congress Catalogue Card Number: 72-109054

I 2 3 4 5 6 7 8 9 — 75 74 73 72 71 70

PRINTED IN THE UNITED STATES OF AMERICA

PARTICIPANTS IN SYMPOSIUM

J. WESLEY ROBB, Ph.D., Professor of Religion, University of Southern California

HENRY WINTHROP, Ph.D., Professor, Department of Interdisciplinary Social Sciences, University of South Florida

HUBERT BONNER, Ph.D., Professor of Psychology, United States International University, California Western University Campus

ORLO STRUNK, JR., Ph.D., Professor of Psychology of Religion, Boston University

SAMUEL A. BANKS, Ph.D., Chaplain and Assistant Professor of Psychiatry and Religion, J. Hillis Miller Center, University of Florida

VIKTOR E. FRANKL, M.D., Ph.D., Professor of Neurology and Psychiatry, Medical School, University of Vienna

WILLIAM DOUGLAS, Ph.D., Lecturer in Psychology, Cape Cod Community College

ARTHUR L. FOSTER, Ph.D., Professor of Theology and Personality, Chicago Theological Seminary

JAMES A. KNIGHT, M.D., Professor of Psychiatry and Associate Dean, Tulane University School of Medicine

JEREMIAH W. CANNING, Ph.D., Associate Professor of Philosophy, Willamette University

DAVID K. SWITZER, Ph.D., Associate Dean of Community Life, Perkins School of Theology, Southern Methodist University

The Religion in Education Foundation acknowledges with appreciation the grants from the Collins Foundation which made possible the two values colloquia from which these papers are drawn.

CONTENTS

VALUES in an AGE OF CONFRONTATION

1

INTRODUCTION

Introduction

JEREMIAH W. CANNING

While gaining historical perspective on past ages often appears as a luxury in our chaotic present, gaining such perspective on the present itself seems more of a crucial necessity. It is axiomatic, of course, that Shakespeare was right in saying that all past is prologue and Santayana right in maintaining that he who fails to understand the past will be condemned to repeat it. Still, there is a definite urgency when we attempt to understand our own age that is not present as we contemplate previous ages. Every age has felt this urgency but the stakes have never before seemed so high. Higher stakes than survival vs. extinction are hard to imagine. So, while it is exciting and often extremely useful to discover the key that seems to unlock an age gone by and transform it from merely a chronological period encompassing certain events to an entire *Weltanchauung*, we had better find the key that unlocks our own age and find it fast, or we will not have to worry about future keys for future locks. Thus we are driven to ponder seriously our own time and search for the insight that will make it intelligible to us. The more we understand what is happening in our world, the more power we will have to change it.

3

If we were to attempt to characterize our own age as we have characterized other ages (the age of faith, the age of enlightment, the age of reason), how would we define it? Suppose we could program a computer to analyze data describing the significant events of our time in such a way that any element common to all could be discovered. What might that element be? Of course, we could play this game in many different ways, depending upon our principle of selection for the events forming the input and the theoretical framework comprising our program. But for heuristic purposes here, let us consider the view that perhaps we live in an age of *confrontation*.

Think of the events which our newspapers headline, our television commentators discuss, and our different art forms try to interpret. None of these events, though current, seem to have *just* happened; they appear to be only the outward symptoms of conditions present for many years. On the international level, Soviet satellite development finds Russian soldiers confronting Czech patriots in the streets of Czechoslovakia's cities; in the Middle East, Israel and her Arab neighbors uneasily confront each other daily across the paper-thin borders perhaps only temporarily separating them; in Viet Nam North confronts South in a hot war, while in Berlin it is East confronting West in a cold war; in South Africa ruling whites confront ruled blacks; and in both Russia and China there are spasmodic shocks as "orthodox believers" confront "liberal revisionists." So, while the nature of these events may be political, racial, religious, or ideological, they are confrontations nonetheless and uniquely indicative of our time.

On the national level as far as the United States is concerned, these characteristics of our age seem even clearer. The Yippies confront the "fuzz" and scream "pigs;" the Vietniks confront "the military-industrial complex" and chant "Hell, no, we won't go;" the Black Militants confront "the white power structure" and raise the spectre of "Burn, baby, burn;" the Hippies confront the "straights" and exhort "Do your own thing;" the clergy of "the new morality" confront "the religious establishment" and proclaim that since its God "is dead," the established church may need to go "underground;" the student activists confront their "multiversities" and threaten to "Grind them to a halt;" and the acid-heads confront the herd-followers and exhort them to "Turn on, tune in, and drop out." Over and over again, then, we see the same process at work, with usually the same result: first alienation and frustration, followed by polarization, and then agitation, ending finally in confrontation.

But *identifying* the problem does not necessarily help us *understand* it. Even if our age may be viewed as an age of confrontation, the really important question is, "Why?" It seems that when the surface of these various confrontations is exposed, what usually is found to lie beneath is a *conflict in values*.

Let us consider some of the examples already mentioned. The Black Militants seem to value a more open way of life for blacks which the whites consider a threat to their own; Peking values an orthodox ideological orientation toward the teachings of Marx which Moscow views as maladaptive to the current demands of the times; the Hippies value a creative individuality which threatens the security of the conformists; the Czechs value a freedom of expression which the Russians feel is dangerous to the unity of Communism; the leaders of the movement for the "underground church" value actual religious experience in the depths of interpersonal relationships which the religious establishment feels would undercut the functioning of the traditional church; Israel values a national way of life which by its very nature the Arab countries consider an offense; and the student activists value a personal and human aspect to education which the multiversity views as inefficient and possibly anarchistic. With such a crisis in values between all these factions, is it any wonder that this crisis would manifest itself in open confrontation? To understand the nature of these different confrontations, then, we need to understand the nature of the value conflicts that underlie them, and it is exactly in the direction of this latter goal that the following papers have been written.

It should be borne in mind that these papers represent the multidisciplinary approach. Such subject areas as psychiatry, theology, sociology, philosophy, anthropology, psychology, education, and religion are all involved, but it is also interesting to note that it is difficult to identify the field of a contributor's specialized training from what he says in his paper. This suggests something about the all-pervasive nature of the concept of value. It is also worth observing that while each man made his own contribution without any preconceived pattern as to which aspect of the value issue he should consider, an examination of the content of the various papers shows how well the various dimensions of the value issue seem to fall into place.

We find Robb and Winthrop mainly analyzing the problem of value on a broad, general level, with the former emphasizing its individual, philosophical aspects, and the latter, its cultural and sociological aspects. Bonner is involved in a bit of confrontation himself as he takes on the present-day "scientific establishment" which he condemns for its lack of concern over the value issues as a legitimate problem for scientific research.

Once the whole idea of research into the value dimension has been broached we find two specific branches of the behavioral sciences being represented. Strunk analyzes psychology specifically and tries to pinpoint problems in research methodology, the philosophy of science underlying such methodology, and the structuring of personality theories based on the application of this methodology. Moving from psychology to psychiatry, Banks' article analyzes various aspects of the value problem as it applies to psychotherapy, both from the standpoint of the therapist's values as well as those of the patient. We then encounter Frankl whose widely-recognized therapy, Logotherapy, actually builds on value-crises rather than attempting to escape them. Douglas follows, giving us an example of what can be undertaken when a psychologist is both concerned and open, as Bonner would like. He presents us with a potential research instrument for use by experimental psychologists in tapping one of the most difficult but most significant of all human variables: value as it relates to religious faith.

Thus far we have mentioned outstanding examples of the types of analyses that would illuminate the value problem on a philosophical and sociological level (Robb and Winthrop); of the kind of defense that would justify the human significance and scientific legitimacy of the problem (Bonner); of the sort of explication of the practical problems encountered in the psychological disciplines attempting to deal with the value issue (Strunk and Banks); and of the kind of creative response that can be brought to these problems (Frankl and Douglas).

But all this would be for naught, of course, if eventually we fail to find our way back to those various areas of confrontation which constitute the very *raison d'être* of all this analysis and research. For after all, the confrontations that threaten to tear apart our own society, as well as the world, are in the areas mentioned earlier and illustrated with examples.

The symposium continues with a look at two of these areas of confrontation, religion and education, in which both analyses of certain problems as well as attempted solutions are given. Foster first points out the importance of an adequate model of man in the understanding of the valuing process, and then analyzes two particular models that posit religious experience as the basis of this process. Knight attempts to apply a model of man to a particular problem of values as they relate to the development of the adolescent. He takes the "new morality" model of man, applies it to this problem, and evaluates its strengths and weaknesses.

Moving from the specific confrontation area of religion to that of education, the paper by the editor is presented as an attempt to come to grips with some of the problematic aspects of education. He analyzes the value commitments that seem to be at the heart of the problem, and tries to point out the ideal strengths as well as the practical weaknesses involved in an alternative set of value commitments for education.

It is fitting, then, to conclude this collection of papers with the one by Switzer, for he illustrates how many of the separate points brought up in the other papers can be integrated into a holistic approach to a given problem. Switzer holds that, as a result of an enlightened philosophy of science, research data exist on the psychological processes involved in the "crisis" periods in an individual's life; further, that psychotherapeutic techniques based on this research have been developed. In addition, Switzer has made an analysis of the basic needs of the individual in the educational setting and offers a partial solution in the form of a "crisis therapy" approach to be incorporated directly into the school systems themselves. Thus, the symposium concludes with a clear-out example of the fruits of the multi-disciplinary approach when applied to the value dimensions of some of the confrontation areas that define our age.

The papers which make up this symposium are presented in a sequential order which is intended to help the reader to get the most out of this particular work. Therefore, these selections, if read in sequence, will be found to hang together logically as a significant *gestalt*. They have been chosen, with this aim in mind, from a series of papers presented by university professors at two Values Colloquia conducted by The Religion In Education Foundation. This agency has been sponsoring scholarly "confrontations" of one kind or another for more than twenty years. Among its services to higher education has been the creation of small, intensive interfield gatherings of scholars for the purpose of exploring provocative ideas in the behavioral and social sciences with regard to the relevance of values to the process of education. The papers in this volume are forerunners of a more extended series. Now that these papers have been released to a wider audience, laymen along with those in the academic community are privileged to investigate in scholarly fashion the various dimensions of the value crises that underlie confrontation.

2

ON MAN AS A VALUING BEING

The Human Quest for Liberation

J. WESLEY ROBB

The cry of man for freedom is not limited to one geographical area of the globe but typifies more and more the mood and temper of our time where men are oppressed and insensitivity to human need prevails. No longer can we extol only the aspirations of men and women in the western world to be free, but the same longing for liberation from the forces of oppression is heard throughout the world. Voznesensky's letter to *Pravda* at the time the Writer's Union refused him permission to read his poetry at a festival in New York in the Spring of 1957 expresses the desire of man for freedom, "I am a Soviet writer, a human being made of flesh and blood, not a puppet to be pulled on a string."

Usually when we think of freedom we identify it with man's social, political, or economic situation. This is very natural due to the emphasis in our cultural understanding upon the role of environment in the development of the individual. From this point of view, if a person lives within a social context that is detrimental to the development of his potentialities as a human being and finds these obstructions to his freedom seemingly impenetrable then he must seek to change the social structure that blocks his development. Stokeley Carmichael takes the position that human freedom has no meaning if the power structure is inimical to the rights of men, particularly, the minorities. He argues that a realistic politics for liberation of the black man in America must include an acceptance of the struggle for power and that in bold terms this means that black power must confront white power in a head-on encounter (2). As a result, the question of human freedom is seen within the setting of the struggle for power and within the context of the social and economic system that causes alienation and estrangement. Black power advocates believe any system must go that breeds inequality and injustice, that protects the privileged status of those in power, and that prohibits self-determination among its people. It is assumed that if power were transferred to other hands, freedom and equality would be realized. This doctrine is nothing new; Karl Marx believed that the change of the economic system would eradicate the social evils that were inherent within the old system and thus liberate man from the chains of economic oppression.

What such sociological and economic analyses of the predicament of man overlook is the problem that man confronts in himself as man. This does not mean that such an awareness should dull our sensitivity to the evils within governmental, economic, or social systems; rather we should focus greater attention upon those causes within man himself that produce the social conditions that limit his freedom for self-expression and fulfillment. In fact, the social situation and the inner condition of man are inseparable. Too long we have assumed that an emphasis upon either the social conditions of man, on the one hand, or stress upon the redirection of the inner self, on the other hand, would resolve the problem. The macrocosm may mirror the microcosm and conversely; the two may be inseparable. However, it is the purpose of this essay to examine the problem of liberating the mind and the spirit of man. We are fully cognizant of the fact that if a man is unemployed and hungry it is nonsense to talk about spiritual liberation. On the other hand, the most affluent societies that assure freedom of movement, freedom of speech, freedom of the press, and the like are some of the most spiritually desolate societies. The evidence of history does not support the thesis that the alleviation of the social ills within a society will automatically create free men in the fullest and richest meaning of that term. We are faced with the stark fact that the most advanced countries in the world in the fields of industry and technology have the highest incidence of suicide, homicide, and alcoholism (3, pp. 8ff.).

The alienated condition of modern man that inevitably leads to personal and social encapsulation is both environmental and existential. That is to say, it is a condition rooted in the very nature of human existence which is aggravated by the nature of the society in which man finds himself. If the problem were purely social and environmental, we could conceivably devise a society where all of the positive qualities of the personality would naturally develop. But in spite of our best efforts, the inner contradiction and ambivalence of our own selves as well as the social paradoxes all about us seem to work against that which we desire to accomplish on a rational plane. This is one of the reasons why students find so much that we do within the academic community irrelevant to either the needs of the society or their own needs as human beings. So little that we do within the formal educational program reaches the sub-corticle level of response and awareness; as the result we are taught to objectify, analyze, and intellectualize while the real problems that disturb us are related to our whole beings as persons involving our emotions, attitudes, and commitments.

It is important to make the distinction between an existential dichotomy and a social dichotomy. An existential dichotomy is a part of the given within the nature of the human condition. For example, man strives towards a level of personal fulfillment that he knows rationally is impossible to achieve; yet it is this constant striving for something higher and better that motivates him in his search for self-realization. He desires to be free, yet no complete freedom is possible within either a society of men or on a personal level as long as he is limited by spatial and temporal reality. I have often thought that man's preoccupation with space travel is perhaps an unconscious attempt to escape the normally experienced limitations of space and time. We seek to become like a god, yet the obvious fact of our finitude and mortality haunts us. All of these paradoxes are a part of the basic reality and nature of our own existence and cannot be escaped. Albert Camus, Erich Fromm, Paul Tillich, and others have made their own statements about these polarities within human experience that seem to foster alienation, estrangement, and anxiety. In contrast, social or environmental dichotomies are those which man creates within his society. For example, poverty and hunger are not unresolvable problems, because man could apply his intelligence to these social ills and eradicate them for the most part. It is much easier to eliminate these kinds of social problems than it is to remove the threat of finitude that man experiences within his own being. It is true that through pharmaceutical agents, normal human response can be eliminated or sedated to the extent that the person does not react to either himself or to the social situation about him. Our previous comments about the condition of man apply to our responses as human beings when we have not been unduly affected by artificial means of altering our personality structure.

Paul Tillich sees the myth of the Fall of Man in the Genesis account as symbolic of the human situation universally. He finds in this story an expression of man's estrangement and the reality of man's finitude. For Tillich, the Fall of Adam illustrates man's finite freedom in which man is both related to and at the same time excluded from infinity to which he belongs. For example, man is free in the way he thinks and speaks; he has the ability to form universals, to think abstractly, and to liberate himself from the bondage of the concrete situation. He is free to ask questions about his own nature and the world of which he is a part, but it is a finite freedom that is limited by his existence in space and time. He is free, yet he is bound. It is man's freedom that makes him different from other things; otherwise he would be a thing among things. The fact that he is free to create or destroy is what makes him distinctly human (10, pp. 29ff.).

Alan Watts identifies the Fall of Man with that point in the evolutionary process where man becomes self-conscious and as the result begins to take himself too seriously. Due to his unique ability to intellectualize, analyze, and think abstractly, man makes himself and his world an object of reflection and thus tends to lose that sensitivity of direct relatedness and feeling he once enjoyed in the Garden of Eden. Watts sees man's inner contradiction as based in his need for knowledge, information, and fact on the one hand, and his need for sensitivity, empathy, and understanding on the other hand (11, pp. 57ff.). Within the context of these needs, man struggles for freedom, wisdom, and insight. The relationship between these values dare not be polarized, but should stand in a relationship of bipolarity and complement to each other.

Therefore, man's quest for liberation must be seen within the context of the human situation marked by finitude, mortality, and limitations of all types. It is an interesting fact that throughout human history there have always been those groups of men as well as brave individuals who have refused to be enslaved or intimidated by either their environment or their own feelings of insecurity. These men and women came to terms with themselves; we call them sages and prophets and their names are legion. Their lives, and in many instances their deaths, illustrate the fact that physical survival should not be identified with true freedom. In an age when high priority is placed upon physical well-being and longevity, it is hard for us to understand that an inner liberation comes even through death. Such commitments to ideal goals may or may not be linked to conventional views of immortality though one might logically argue that a commitment to an ideal value may have some ontological significance. What matters is what happens within the soul of man as he sacrifices for an end that he believes is worthy of his supreme loyalty. The confidence and self-assurance that Socrates manifested as he drank the hemlock in a prison cell in Greece demonstrates this kind of power for self-transcendence. The lucidity of Martin Luther King in his final address the day prior to his murder demonstrates the power of the human spirit to reach a level of freedom from fear and illustrates a kind of freedom that defies both the ambivalence of man's own nature and the limitations of space and time. It bears within it an eternal quality to which we intuitively respond.

The problem is that most men are encapsulated and do not recognize it, or recognize it only in those moments of self-reflection, or in the presence of examples of great men who have discovered what freedom really means. We live in cages and as the result tend to lose our identity as individual selves or persons. Rollo May relates the parable about the man who was put in a cage (7, Chap. 11). It seems that a tyrannical king was seized with the idea of what would happen if a man were kept in a cage. So he called in the palace psychologist and asked him to perform the experiment. At first, the psychologist objected on the grounds that it was inhumane; but when the king told him that he had received a grant from the Greater Social Research Foundation the psychologist agreed to the experiment. A cage was brought into the courtyard of the palace and an unsuspecting subject of the kingdom was kidnapped by the palace guards and put in the cage.

At first, the man was so bewildered he did not know how to react but as soon as he became aware of his plight he began to protest vigorously. Each day the king came to visit him and to reassure him that his life was not bad at all, that he had good food, a comfortable place to stay, medical attention, and other benefits. In fact, he was better off than many other people. In time, the reassurances of the king seemed persuasive and the psychologist observed that the prisoner was constructing theories about the legitimacy of his situation and that all men needed food and shelter. He had come to accept his situation, but his voice lacked feeling and conviction. However, the psychologist noticed that when he was alone he was often sullen and morose and that when he talked about his situation he no longer used the personal pronoun, but only said, "It is fate." He had accepted his enslavement; he, as a person with identity, no longer existed because he had lost both his external and, more fundamentally, his internal freedom.

In a sense all men are in a cage and though the parable is extreme in its form, it does illustrate the plight every man faces who resists conformity and seeks true self-identity. The point at which the man in the cage began to break down occurred when his protests ceased and he began to construct formal defenses for the legitimacy of his situation, even to the point of accepting his fate without a protest, a whimper, or a murmur. It is this phenomenon of accepting our fate without a protest that is so disturbing about the middle-class American who is so surrounded with gadgets and devices to make him comfortable and secure that he voices little or no protest no matter how grievous the offense might be. He is silent about international affairs; he refuses to be involved in the debate about capital punishment; he closes his eyes and ears to the problems of poverty; he is fearful about any critical examination of the status quo; he runs for cover when the going gets tough in the social and political arenas. He is well fed, has a good bed, and has accepted his closed off and provincial world as the real world. He thinks he is happy, as did the man in the cage, either because he never knew the difference between enslavement and freedom or because he does not want to leave the womb of security and enter the uncertain world of feeling, conviction, and freedom. He is a member of those exclusive clubs where Negroes and Jews are not welcome, where wealth and power are the marks of value rather than creativity, spontaneity, and intellectuality. He views morality in terms of nationalism—a patriotism that is uncritical of government or external fidelity—an appearance of loyalty, trust, and faith, while at the same time he is involved in special business deals that return an unwarranted dividend through someone else's misfortune. He adheres to the letter of the law, but he has forgotten what justice, mercy, and humility mean. He is a slave and does not know it; he is bound by his own condition and is anxious to bring others into the cage with him. He lives in what E. E. Cummings calls "a not alive undead too nearishness." He has lost spontaneity in living; its excitement is gone. He has lost his freedom.

Modern man has lost his zest for living, the kind of experience that children express in their own exuberant, uninhibited way. Albert Camus expresses his nolstalgia about the experiences and images of childhood when he says, "Yes, only to capture the transparency and simplicity of paradises lost—in an image" (1, p. 37). For an adult to recapture such lucidity and innocence would be to threaten the artificiality and formality of the life we lead and with which we surround ouselves in the name of propriety. But when propriety forces sterility of form and expression, and the vision of paradise is gone, then the personality shrinks into perhaps an acceptable form, but one that no longer reaches its potential for love and creativity. It is within this context that the Hippies and Beatniks have scored a direct hit! These people may appear to be fun-loving no-goods, but their restlessness is caused, to a great degree, by their disillusionment with modern society as they find it. Since they do not find a niche in society where they fit, they resort to extreme forms of self-expression in an attempt to find their identity. Their search for meaning, freedom, and frequently self-gratification carries an intellectual and spiritual sensitivity which generally is misunderstood by a middle class society that has sated itself with good things and little pleasures but refuses to face the fundamental questions about human existence. The search for a "happening" within the life of our young people, most of whom are not the extremists of the Allen Ginsberg variety, is a quest for a type of experience that will take the individual outside the normal range of his experience into a new world of wonder and excitement and hopefully, meaning. Such attempts for a new experience are searches for "self-insight, a realization of customarily obscured immensities, and an acceptance—in the existential sense—of the ongoing moment" (9, p. 32).

Timothy Leary suggests five dilemmas which psychedelic "happenings" arouse and, I would suggest, at many points parallel the motivation behind the quest for spiritual freedom that has characterized the lives of mystics and saints throughout the ages. (1) The *fear* of a loss of rational control is balanced by the *hope* of transcending habitual patterns of life and freeing oneself to new levels of awareness. (2) The *fear* of seeing oneself as one really is and the *hope* of finding one's true self. (3) The *fear* of total cynicism about society and where the individual fits within it and the *hope* of insight into the true nature of the social process with the added wisdom that will bring creative action. (4) The *fear* of discovering a realm of experience so pleasant that one will not want to return to the real world and the *hope* that one can reach a level of experience that will transform his world into one of splendor. (5) The *fear* of acting in a shameful manner and the *hope* that one will act as one truly wants to act without being bound by the fetters of society and tradition (9, pp. 50-51. The numberings are Robb's.).

Note the aspirations and hopes in each case. The hope of self-transcendence; the hope of finding one's true self; the hope of new insight into the nature of life and the world; the hope of transforming one's world into paradise and splendor; and the hope of doing and being what one really wants to be. These desires of the human spirit constitute a cry for freedom.

Is this desire for freedom innate? Is it characteristic of the human species regardless of social forces that would enslave man? Perhaps Dostoevsky gives us the answer. In *Notes from Underground* the literary genius speaks of the innate desire on the part of man to be more than "keys of a piano" or "stops on an organ." He points out that though man be given all earthly blessings possible, he still would retain his right to choose certain values for himself and use his affluence toward those ends he deems in his own interest. And why? "Simply to prove to himself—as though that were necessary—that men still are men. . . . And this is not all," he adds, "even if man were really nothing but a piano key, even if this were proved to him by natural science and mathematics, even then he would not become reasonable, but would purposely do something perverse out of simple ingratitude, simply to gain his point" (12, pp. 205-6).

To approach scientifically the subjective fact of our own self-intuition that we possess a modicum of self-determination and freedom is to rely upon a methodology that is not only inadequate but inappropriate (8). By "scientific" I mean a radical empiricism that insists upon public and objective verifiability as the basis for its claim. If, however, one includes within the scope of his concern the data of human experience and the operational assumptions upon which reflective man acts and assumes within the behavioral patterns of others, then an empirical approach within a broader and more inclusive understanding of the term, can be applied. History is replete with the stories of individuals and groups who refused to be subject to an oppressive political, religious, or economic system and who challenged those who would attempt to conquer their spirits by offering their own lives as a sacrifice to the reality of those principles they believed to be of ultimate value.

Perhaps the freedom we seek stands in relationship to a trans-cultural dimension of our existence. It is no happenstance that human love has been described by writers, artists, and composers throughout human history as being in some way rooted in the very nature of existence itself. This is why we resort to poetic and artistic symbols to express the meaning of those experiences that seem to point to a referent far richer in meaning and significance than that which dominates our mundane life. It is a freedom of the inner self that expresses itself not "because of" but "in spite of," and gives us the courage to realize our being as we experience "Being" in the reality of its depth, richness, and all pervasiveness. Reason and observation are limited in their perspective; they tend to truncate our existence into models of experience that encapsulate us. Man stands within the stream of a given culture at a given time and place in history; yet, at the same time he stands above culture in his ability to dream of the future and in his intuitive awareness that his own sense of presence in human relationships is grounded in a a transcendent "Presence."

Gabriel Marcel develops this theme by pointing out that "at the root of presence there is a being who takes me into consideration, who is regarded by me as taking me into account...Presence as response to the act by which the subject opens himself to receive; in this sense it is the gift of oneself. Presence belongs only to the being who is capable of giving himself." And then he adds, "I must ask myself what an eternal, indefectible presence would be" (6, p. 153).

Marcel suggests that interpersonal relationships are the doorway to an understanding of the mystery of Being as the divine presence within human life. This awareness of the meaning of presence on both the human and ontic levels of experience opens new avenues for the experience and meaning of freedom. The exuberation, exhilaration, and liberating influence of such experiences enables man to face tragedy, despair, and disappointment. Professor Sam Keen (5) points out that Marcel explored very early in his career the metaphysical significance of various modes of relationships. He made such distinctions as an "I" and a "thou" vs. an "I" and a "he" relationship—distinctions which have become a part of the common theological and philosophical vocabulary since the publication of Martin Buber's works. Both Marcel and Buber see the metaphysical implications of genuine human relationships that bear upon the human condition within the concrete situation within which man finds himself.

Religion has played a somewhat paradoxical role in liberating the spirit of man. There have been times in history when religious beliefs have stifled creative and free thought; when dogma and authority dominated the intellectual life of man; when crusades in the name of religion have forfeited human life as though it were a pawn on the divine chessboard of history; when religious sanctions have been used to preserve privilege, class, and caste; when men have assumed a chosen relationship to deity and as the result have invoked divine blessing upon causes that were nationalistic in purpose and scope; when tradition insisted on its own self-authenticating character to be left unexamined and uncriticized.

But this is not the whole story. Religion has also played a constructive role in freeing the spirit of man to rise above the mood or temper of the time facing even death with equanimity and calm repose. Collective expressions of religious belief have tended

to be fixed in the cement of tradition and authority while individual
expressions of religious faith and practice have often broken through
the narrow and hidebound ways of understanding and expression
to cast a basic truth into a new and living mold. Such personal
testimonies to the liberating power of the spirit have usually been
grounded in a depth of religious feeling and experience that bore
with it its own self-authenticity. The hymns of faith, for example,
within the Christian Church are not rational attempts to defend the
legitimacy of their message; they are proclamations of faith bear-
ing within themselves a supporting logic that needs no external
defense. Recent trends in linguistic analysis have recognized the
legitimacy of religious language in poetry and song and ritual as
having cognitive meaning for those standing within the community
of faith where these forms are used. Thus the liberating influence
and power of faith is seen within the context of a community of
faith that gives sustenance and strength to him who believes. Such
faith has been always viewed as a gift, as grace, as a miracle in
which the whole cosmos broadens and deepens in richness and
fullness. It is a venture of trust responding to the threat of despair.

To assume that the liberation of the spirit was possible in any
absolute sense would be to falsify the human situation. The Early
Church Fathers were consistent in their claim that the beatific
vision came in the life to come. We are creatures of sense and
spirit; man lives in a two-dimensional world; therefore, man must
not expect too much. There is the reality of tragedy, despair, and
loneliness about life that is a part of the given just as the existential
dichotomies, mentioned earlier in this essay, are a part of the nature
of what is. One of the reasons for the rebellion against religion is
the too facile answer and the glib twist of the written and spoken
word. This is why the existentialism of Camus and Sartre appeals
to the contemporary mind because it does not sweep the absurdity
and meaningless nature of life under the philosophical or theological
rug. Each espouses in his own way a rugged individualism that
sees hope only in the searching and questing mind and spirit of
man that refuses to be bludgeoned into submission. This is a part
of the humanistic tradition that has its roots within the Judeo-
Christian and Greek culture of western man. What such a view
denies is the sustaining power of the universe of which man is a
part. If the universe is silent to man's fate, then Camus is right, but

the hope of religion is centered within the faith that man is finite, inadequate, and helpless to redeem himself, that he is overbuilt for this world and that the cosmic dimension of his being is as much a fact of his existence as his temporality and finitude.

The Judeo-Christian and the secular humanistic approach to life are responses of faith and both include a mystic quality about them. One is centered in that mystery of the power of human relationships that can enable us to transcend and transform the present while the other sees this human quality of self-transcending power as being related to another dimension of reality and existence —other than the solely human or environmental.

Albert Schweitzer expressed a religious approach to life, meaning, and freedom when he wrote, "I live my life in God, in the mysterious ethical divine personality which I cannot discover in the world, but only experience in myself as a mysterious impulse" (4, p. 260).

REFERENCES

1. Camus, Albert, *Lyrical and Critical Essays*. New York: Alfred A. Knopf, Inc., 1968.

2. Carmichael, Stokeley and Charles V. Hamilton, *Black Power*. New York: Random House, Inc., 1967.

3. Fromm, Erich, *The Sane Society*. New York: Holt, Rinehart & Winston, Inc., 1955.

4. Joy, Charles R., ed., *Albert Schweitzer: An Anthology*. Boston: Beacon Press, 1947.

5. Keen, Sam, *Gabriel Marcel*. Richmond, Va.: John Knox Press, 1957.

6. Marcel, Gabriel, *Presence and Immortality*. Pittsburgh: Duquesne University Press, 1967.

7. May, Rollo, *Psychology and the Human Dilemma*. New York: Van Nostrand Reinhold Company, 1967.

8. Ramsey, Ian, ed., *Biology and Personality*. Oxford, England: Basil Blackwell, 1965. One of the central themes of this volume is that of human freedom. Here outstanding scientists, philosophers, and theologians discuss the problem of the nature of man. This book illustrates the point I have just made, namely, that scientific evidence

does not in itself coerce a man to believe or disbelieve in the reality of the freedom of the human spirit.

9. Simmons, J. J. and Barry Winograd, *It's Happening*. Santa Barbara, Cal.: Marc Laird Publications, 1966.

10. Tillich, Paul, *Systematic Theology*, Vol. II. Chicago: University of Chicago Press, 1957.

11. Watts, Alan, *Beyond Theology*. New York: Random House, Inc., 1964.

12. Yarmolinsky, A., ed., *The Three Short Novels of Dostoevsky*. New York: Doubleday & Company, Inc., 1960.

THE HUMAN QUEST FOR LIBERATION

Editorial Comments

In Robb's article we encounter a distinction that must be one of the most basic of all the distinctions with respect to the confrontation/value issue. He distinguishes between man's external, social situation, and his individual, inner condition, although observing that they are interdependent and thus not really separable except for purposes of analysis. Expanding upon his application of this distinction to the general area of confrontation, we can see that logically, as well as historically, there have been three main types of responses to the various value conflicts that underlie different confrontations.

First, one could focus entirely on the social situation and attempt solely to undermine those institutions perpetuating the values one wished to negate. Our present day Yippies would seem a good example of a group dedicated to this approach, with soul-searching at a minimum and social agitation at a maximum. On the international level the Arab attitude toward Israel would also appear to be one where the focus was not on transcending the value conflict in a psychological sense, but in eliminating the basis for the conflict in a sociological sense.

Second, one could withdraw from the social aspects of the problem and devote one's energies to improving the self rather than society. Followers of the Maharishi Meshesh Yoga may benefit India with a "social fallout" as a result of their psychological transformations at some future time, but the focus at the present is on the individual self that transcendentally meditates rather than the individual self that agitates for social reform. And those in our own country who are dedicated to "the expanding of human consciousness" via the hallucinogenic route also seem committed to the second type of approach. The "turning on" and "tuning in" one is supposed to do are definitely of an internal and individual psychological nature, while the dropping out part seems to refer to the social arena where the institutions exist which represent the values that constitute the basis for the conflict. One is not to destroy these institutions but merely to walk away from them.

The third approach one could adopt, of course, combines the active element from each of the other two. In this approach one would attempt to transform the social order as well as the self. The recent history of India furnishes us with a clear example of this type of situation, for Gandhi certainly was a revolutionary in the sense of one wishing to tear down the *status quo* and yet he was also a spiritual man committed to non-violence and constantly striving to perfect the state of his soul. A parallel example from our own country can be found in the Black Power movement of today, although the shift from a context of non-violence to one of violence would tend to obfuscate this parallelism for many. Nevertheless, what other meaning could one give to the dual slogans of the movement, "Burn, baby, burn" and "Black is beautiful," than that the social institutions that perpetuate the black's economic, educational, and political enslavement must be "burned down" and that the individual black man must psychologically transcend the "ugly" image of himself that the white man has so effectively taught him and substitute for it a "beautiful" image of his own.

Using Robb's distinction, then, we see three main possible responses to the types of value confrontations we have been discussing. Robb chooses to focus his attention mainly on the personal side. The crucial importance of investigating the social side as well may now be seen in the following article by Winthrop.

3

ON MAN'S SOCIAL MATRIX

The Contemporary Problem of Moral Complexity

HENRY WINTHROP

The Historical, Common Purpose of Liberal Education

At certain stages in the history of education it has been emphasized that the *ultimate objective* of a liberal education is to make men take seriously the question of what constitutes the good life. This question appears in the form of how to discriminate between prospectively good and bad actions—actions which are intended to deal with the issues of social importance and whose social consequences can likewise promote good or evil. Recognition of these matters as the basic, common goals of a liberal education is without prejudice to the goals of specialization and to those skills and that informational content in the curriculum which should be part of the intellectual acquisition of all.

Aristotle recognized that it is impossible to be wise without being good, and impossible to be good without being wise. Being good means being effectively moral and, broadly speaking, this means exemplifying in a thousand and one concrete actions in specific contexts, the four cardinal virtues of courage, temperance, justice, and prudence. But even the brightest and most well-intentioned of us cannot just choose to be moral. Nor can we be taught in higher education various formulas by which we can learn to distinguish between good and bad actions. What men call moral behavior and good character are virtues which can come only from much and varied experience—experience that has been *deeply* reflected upon. Subjects that require experience do not convey their full meaning to the inexperienced.

In this sense, at best we can expect of the young "good moral habits" which are learned from their elders, without such habits necessarily being the product of reflection. It is only from those who are no longer young that one has the right to expect moral sensitivities, moral postures, and moral actions, for the required experience which *may* generate these can come, of course, only with the passage of time. Clearly neither experience nor age will guarantee the wisdom to be good. They are the *necessary conditions* for a personally and publicly effective morality. They are, however, in no sense the *sufficient conditions*. Men also have to reflect deeply upon their experience.

In addition, men have to feel keenly the emotional significance of what they, themselves, and others besides have gone through in order to derive the lesson such experience has for the achievement of grace and virtue. This process of derivation is part of what is meant by wisdom. Its object is to avoid looking at the lives and plights of others too abstractly. Wisdom can never be a good neighbor to alienation. But experience whose *emotional import* has never been sought, which is never reflected upon for significance, and which rarely serves to establish a sense of lasting value for the individual, is meaningless experience. It is "empty" experience and most of the world's citizens throughout history have gone to their graves on a diet of empty experience.

When Aristotle lays down the dictum that in order to be wise one must be good and in order to be good one must be wise, he is speaking to us across the centuries, from a time in which the social environments and communities which men had created for themselves were simple in nature and relatively easy to understand. A man pressed for a decision in a Greek city-state was a man presented with only a few choices and in a milieu which an intelligent citizen could hope to understand. Further than this, if he sought to anticipate the consequences of any course of action he might choose to take, he had an excellent chance of being able to do so, because the consequences he sought to foresee would be generated by the interaction of his behavior with relatively simple, institutional artifacts. Thus he could really hope to be able to count both personal and social costs.

But this is no longer so in the modern world. Men now face a world of such social complexity that if our mythical Greek freeman could be returned from the dead and asked to function in his new environment with all the personal and civic virtue he was able to muster in the old, he would find himself confronted with difficulties of a hair-raising nature. In the first place any issue he faced would be bristling with a wider variety of choices than he had ever encountered before. Most of these choices would intrinsically be more difficult to deal with than those to which he had grown accustomed in his essentially agrarian milieu. In the second place, the analytic task of trying to foresee the modes of interaction between his prospective behavior and the institutions of the community would be so greatly increased that he would be bound to overlook many of the significant points of intersection. This is because our socially more complex world today consists of literally hundreds of institutions which may affect our behavior, so that the task of relating one's behavior to one's world calls for more knowledge, more patience and more thought than our Greek might be prepared to strive for.

Third, the manner in which our behavior can interact with existing institutions is not easily seen. To understand such interaction a vast amount of detailed knowledge of technical procedures and rules and regulations is necessary, something which our mythical Greek might balk at acquiring once the necessity was pointed out to him. Last and most important of all, the technique of trying to prevision the personal and social consequences of each of our actions in a complex social system like ours—with its many interdependencies and interlockings—is well nigh impossible. This is why planning is becoming increasingly difficult in our time and that is why the dilemmas it presents—which were so forcefully dealt with by Jewkes (11)—still remain largely unsolved. Even if the complex social system within which moral decisions had to be made were stable—and this is exactly what it is not, since, as Boulding (2) has pointed out, it is constantly being subjected to system breaks—it is becoming almost impossible to work out many of the important reverberations of any new actions taken within such a complex system. If men have a limited grasp of the complex social system in which they find themselves, they cannot escape the necessity of acting blindly, to some degree, within that system. This "partial blindness" means, in effect, that it is almost presumptuous to talk about trying to foresee most of the personal and social effects of one's actions on groups remote from us in space and circumstances. Counting costs is now more a desideratum than an accomplishable fact.

In what sense, then, does our world of social complexity lead to a world of such moral complexity that Aristotle's dictum has great difficulty in obtaining a foothold? In the section which follows I shall try to answer this question and in the last section I shall try to state briefly in what ways modern higher education can contribute to the alleviation of the moral perplexities of our age.

Some Aspects of Moral Complexity

If a citizen wishes to be all of a piece, morally speaking, he finds himself in difficulties of a kind which are generally uncontrollable and unmanageable. If he wishes to support the kind of community which he feels would bring happiness, security, and the promise of personal development for most of us, he has no guidelines in the face of the social complexity of our age. There are fundamentally two types of moral inconsistency which straitjacket the morally sincere person today. One is the inconsistency which results from inescapable, self-defeating action. The other is the inconsistency which results from not knowing the moral consequences which result from many of our actions. Unfortunately, left to his own devices, the average citizen is not likely to do the kind of thinking and show the kind of concern by means of which he can steer clear of the shoals of moral inconsistency. Given an opportunity, however, to become aware of both the nature of moral dilemmas and the kind of discourse which is suited to the task of dealing honestly with such dilemmas, the citizen will find that modes of awareness are opened up to him which heretofore may have escaped him entirely. If the average citizen can be helped to unite a

sense of the social complexity of the modern community with a
sense of the urgent need to apply a moral posture to the problems
generated by that complexity, a good deal of personal and com-
munal error can be avoided. The modern university can be of un-
questionable assistance in exercising some relatively novel functions
which are aimed at beginning the job of liquidating the current dimensions of our moral complexity. In the next section I shall try to
state briefly some of the ways in which higher education can contribute to the understanding and relief of the situation with which I
am here concerned.

Higher Education and the Contemporary Problem of Modern Complexity

There is available today quite a roster of techniques which are
relevant to the task of facilitating the individual's ability to deal
with moral complexity. To the extent that moral dilemmas are due
to lack of self-awareness or to blunted social perception and insensitivity towards the psychological needs and makeup of other people, certain ameliorative methods are today available—methods
which will increase awareness and fellow-feeling. Such persons as
Jack and Lorraine Gibbs (8, pp. 161-70) on the one hand, and
Weschler and Reisel (16) on the other, have given us brief but
insightful descriptions of some of the methods involved. Regimes
for the promotion of social altruism and social love—in terms of the
awakening of social and religious concern—have been described by
Sorokin (14). The fields of clinical psychology and psychiatry
have developed dozens of new types of therapy for dealing with
various types of psychological blocs. These, *in part*, can substantially
increase our sense of moral awareness and moral complexity—if we
are bent in that direction. Some of these novel types of psychotherapy have been brought together for us by Bychowski and
Despert (3).

Techniques of disalienation, which can considerably increase
moral awareness, are helped by "milieu therapy"—that is, by plung-
ing morally insensitive individuals, who are extremely alienated in
some sense, into life contexts which will "open their eyes" and provide that quality of essential experience which kindles moral awak-

ening. The capacity for moral arousal is something the printed word so often lacks. For those who by disposition can act on enlightened principle and for whom an abstract intellectual approach sometimes proves serviceable, one can resort to a discussion involving a *dialectic of morals*, such as that provided by Mortimer Adler (1). Finally, the techniques of extensional orientation, which the general semanticists have stressed for decades, can increase situational awareness and derivately to some extent, moral perception. Dubois (7) has called our attention to some of these.

There are many other techniques—both psychological and non-psychological in nature—which, in one way or another, are relevant to the task of increasing our sense of moral complexity and moral awareness. This is not the place to draw up a roster of such techniques. What I wish to concentrate upon here is the use of three nonpsychological techniques for increasing our sense of moral complexity and, hopefully and derivatively arousing our sense of moral concern. These three techniques are the following: 1) Techniques which restore a sense of the value and the usefulness of contextual moral discourse. The adjective "contextual" is used here to contrast a moral dilemma, posed in a real situation, with one posed abstractly and solely in verbal terms, in terms of logical structure, or in terms of mathematical analysis. 2) Techniques which will deal with social complexity by educating people to the meaning of the "concept of coordination" in social and economic planning (18). In this way individuals may acquire a deep sense of the structual difficulties involved in this type of decision-making and experience intellectually the full range of moral inconsistency prevalent in the social pathology of our time. 3) Programs which acquaint people with the extent to which moral and social complexity are a function of large-scale community life. Such programs will have to make abundantly clear the extent to which a philosophy of decentralization, along with a sophisticated use of recent developments in science and technology can provide the type of small-scale community which will considerably reduce both social and moral complexity. If these are reduced we can then expect derivatively a reduction in moral inconsistency, both for individuals as well as for groups. Let me, then, turn to a discussion of each of these three techniques.

One of the first things which a modern and streamlined version of liberal education can do to meet the difficulties dealt with in the preceding section is to restore respect and appreciation for, as well as understanding of, moral discourse itself. In particular, we need to make the undergraduate aware of the relevance of such discourse for the problems of our age and for contemporary issues which are generating storms of partisan controversy that are conspicuous for their moral ambiguities. The need for discussion in a moral context has been neglected—if it has not, in fact, become highly unpopular—as the spirit of scientism has increasingly invaded the halls of learning. I am not here assuming that such discourse will inculcate moral attitudes and moral behavior. That would be absurd. These things, as we have already said, cannot be taught. What I am saying, however, is that the undergraduate needs to be *sensitized* to the merits of moral attitudes and moral behavior, particularly for the specific contexts of social controversy in our time. It is the *sensitivity*, as such, that we must seek. After that we can only hope that when the undergraduate becomes a citizen participating in the solutions of the problems faced in his community, he will be prompted, by virtue of his previous training, to take a *moral stance* towards such problems.

This does not mean just striking a moral posture. It means engaging in moral analysis and welcoming the necessity of accompanying that analysis by the expression of those types of mature feeling which are proper to it and are *part* of the *sine qua nons* of authentic, moral analysis. It is this type of communication—whether engaged in as an internal examination or pursued in a dialogue with others—which is so strikingly absent from the atmosphere of higher education today—at least in the social sciences. This absence is recognized by certain writers who have made efforts to plug the gap. I am thinking in this connection of the work of Schoock and Wiggins (13), Girvetz (9), Szasz (15), and De George (6). But such work has hardly begun to make a dent in the moral hollowness of the moribund, liberal tradition which permeates most of higher education today.

There is a second way in which higher education can contribute to the liquidation of the moral impasses of our time. In the social planning and management sciences and in our departments of philosophy, we need to set time aside to demonstrate the many ways in which the social complexity of our age conditions the atmosphere of moral decision. In addition, we also need to point out the many ways in which moral complexity arises and the many ways in which moral inconsistency can occur. This is a large order and yet it can be done rather well today, if we are so-minded. That is because the groundwork for doing so has been well laid by other disciplines which have until now only skirted moral issues. What I wish to point out in this connection is that there exists a vast pool of material in the disciplines I have just mentioned which lends itself to bringing moral issues into focus. Thus, if we make use of a volume which deals with proposed alternative solutions to our social problems—like that of Gold and Scarpitti (10)—we can state, side by side with each of the proposed solutions, the moral issues which are involved. These issues can then be examined in relation to: 1) our notions of the good life, 2) the extent to which the proposed solutions facilitate or inhibit these notions, 3) the extent to which the solutions to different problems work at cross-purposes (moral inconsistency), 4) the kinds of consequences which we can prevision for some of the proposed solutions, and 5) the desirability or undesirability of such anticipated consequences.

An approach of this sort makes moral discourse completely relevant to the social issues of our time and brings that relevancy into focus for many students. Using this technique, what would otherwise be regarded as a metaphysical luxury is seen to be quite germane to the controversies which are currently polarizing individuals and groups. It takes a knowledgeable, thoughtful, concerned, and imaginative teacher to do this sort of thing, to be sure, but this is the perfect demonstration in dialogue of what is meant by the Aristotelian dictum—that it is impossible to be wise without being good and impossible to be good without being wise. Similar opportunities exist when discussing planning techniques, management problems in government and industry, and conflicts in political philosophy. In present practice, these are all largely "missed possibilities" but it would not be very difficult intrinsically to revamp the curriculum in each of these fields so as to include at least one course which will do these things—preferably taught in an interdisciplinary fashion—and which will result in *sensitizing* the undergraduate to the *atmosphere of moral concern*.

This concern can always be separately distinguished *intellectually* from *moral commitment in action*. The latter is what the French mean when they say the individual is *engagé*. But we must refuse to be spiritual gluttons with respect to this issue. We must be satisfied if we can *provoke* concern and if we can hope, democratically and morally, that the individual will subsequently give *expression* to his concern *in action*. We must not command that action from others and we must not deride its absence. It is the task of higher education, however, to nourish it.

Lastly, there is a third way in which modern higher education can contribute to the alleviation of the moral dilemmas of our time. This is a way that involves the recognition that social complexity leads to moral complexity, and that moral complexity leads to moral dilemmas and inconsistencies. It is very difficult to think of ways and means for defeating those aspects of our sick society which have their roots in the social complexity which men have now created for themselves. There may be a practical way, however, in which man can undo these trends. If men make a deliberate effort to simplify the nature of community, that is, to decentralize physically and institutionally—in such a way as to retain most of the *advantages* now associated erroneously with *urbanization*—this may prove to be a way out. Decentralization means less social complexity and less social complexity reduces error and ignorance. Less social complexity also increases significantly the possibility of personal and moral control over events and enlarges the opportunity for the expression of social responsibility.

The simplification which decentralization calls for is not to be mistakenly interpreted as a call for a return to the pastoral simplicity which Tolstoi consistently preached. It is rather a simplicity of organization and structure which can prevail within the context of social and welfare opportunities provided by an age of science and technology. Whether men will seek to give serious thought and practical expression to such a way out remains to be seen. It may, however, be the optimal way out if we can only free ourselves of the unquestioned and unchallenged notion that urbanization and bureaucratization—the excesses in our time which have grown from obsession with bigness and large-scale thinking—are the inescapable trends of the future.

The morally sensitive educator can contribute to the task just mentioned by pointing out in the classroom the types of social and moral problems which a socially complex, mass society generates and the moral difficulties in the way of solving such problems. In contrast, he should also make it his business to show how the small-scale but modernized, decentralized community can succeed in avoiding problems of this type. In addition, he can also point out extensively the greater ease with which social and moral problems can be handled in the small-scale community and the somewhat different types of moral issues which the small-scale community produces. Above all, he can show fairly conclusively, I think, the reduced danger of moral inconsistency in the less complex, decentralized community. And, finally, the intellectual and moral yield is quite satisfying when the instructor can show the many kinds of pathological behavior which take easy root in mass society—a task which has been ably carried out to some extent by Ludwig (12).

It should be pointed out here that the quest for decentralized but modernized communities as one means of *preventing the appearance* of social and moral complexity—what I have elsewhere called the scientific, intentional micro-community (18, pp. 74-97)— is completely opposed to an outlook which has recently made quite a stir in certain theological circles. I am referring to the doctrine of secularization made prominent by Harvey Cox (5) and others (4). Cox is a theologian who is convinced that the modern, highly industrialized and bureaucratized urban center—the technopolis or secular city, to use his expressions—is the wave of the future. Cox feels that the large urban center offers potentially the best institutional advantages and characteristics for expressing the affirmative religious impulse through the Social Gospel. He asks us to reject the typical criticisms of the metropolis, offered by intellectuals and social critics in our time, and to regard them as mistaken. Cox sees the rejection of our modern conurbations as a rejection based upon the anti-urban bias of social critics—poverty-stricken in imagination—who have missed all the creative potentialities for authentic human relations offered by the metropolis.

This is not the place, of course, to launch into a detailed description of what I take to be the mistakes of Cox, the "urbophile." Here I only wish to emphasize the following points: 1) Cox overlooks or plays down the social pathologies which may be inextricably associated with urban bigness, 2) he is almost completely unaware of the extent to which that urban bigness generates the social and ecological complexities of our age, 3) he shows no realization of the interlocking of social complexity and the moral complexities men now face in social evaluation and decision-making, and 4) he has ignored the alternative of up-to-date scientific and technological decentralization as expressible in potentially small-scale community life.

In order, then, to streamline a philosophy of decentralization for modern man, a teacher will have to be quite knowledgeable and socially well informed. He most certainly will have to be familiar with the major historical criticisms of centralism, urbanization and bureaucracy. He will also surely have to be familiar with philosophies of decentralization and with the sociological research findings concerning the advantages of small-scale community. There will be many other things he will have to know, of course, besides these. But they will all be relevant to the task of showing students the extent to which decentralization cuts down social complexity and, derivatively, moral complexity and moral inconsistency. Such knowledge will have to be an essential prerequisite for the instructor who hopes to make meaningful the task of sensitizing the undergraduate to the moral concerns of the age. It is not an easy task to acquire such knowledge or to exhibit moral concern in the classroom. But for the teacher—alive to the moral issues which are coming more and more into focus in Western society—it is better to wrestle with these difficulties and fail than not to have tried at all. The teacher's failure may be followed by a pupil's success sometime later. But if the teacher shuns the task altogether, then we clearly have the case in which intellectual ease has been purchased at the expense of repressing the moral sense. Such repression is not worth the social cost it creates.

We should not close this discussion without a reminder of the fact that there are positive factors which lend themselves to sensitizing the undergraduate to the importance of a personal morality, a public philosophy, and the need to achieve a community consensus on what constitutes the good life. All three of these considerations have received expression in the spate of books which, in recent years, have dealt with ferment on the campus. Numerous scholars have also lost no time in trying to analyze the youth movement throughout the world and in dealing with the moral and ethical dimensions of the personal and social issues that have given rise to the passionate criticism of Western society, on the part of the young. The social and behavioral sciences have also made their contributions. These have occurred in the attempts to relate the findings of the different disciplines to the pressing social issues of our time. Psychologists have done research which has influenced national legislation dealing with segregation. Anthropologists have helped to lessen American provincialism through objective analyses of American culture and regional and occupational subcultures. Sociologists have been pitiless in subjecting social inequities, injustices, class and group prejudices, national values, and political corruption to the moments of truth demanded by scientific method and social concern. Thinkers and innovators in religion have been quick to come to grips with the hypocrisies and rationalizations which take shelter within religious credos and institutions. The social gospel has been given a splendid rebirth—one which has succeeded effectively in distinguishing between the religious impulse, on the one hand, and loyalty to theological credos, denominational clannishness and mere churchgoing, on the other.

All this spiritual and intellectual ferment is precisely part of a tract for the times. All of it is slowly producing guidelines for men and women who seek to be true to the religious impulse in the present and to the obligations and responsibilities due posterity the day after tomorrow. The teacher who seeks to keep his pact with man, the teacher who seeks to deal honestly with the secular trends we have emphasized above, the teacher who adds his efforts to the task of helping men to be of one piece, socially and morally, can draw upon all the sources of secular and spiritual wisdom which are part of the wave of the future. In doing so, he makes himself morally responsible. Such a commitment helps the undergraduate to realize the great, Greek, educational ideal of *paideia*—self-fulfillment and civic responsibility. Out of such involvement comes the nobility of man.

REFERENCES

1. Adler, Mortimer, "A Dialectic of Morals," in *The Review of Politics*. Notre Dame, Indiana: University of Notre Dame Press, 1941.

2. Kenneth E. Boulding has discussed the concept of a "system break" in the paper, "Looking Ahead to the Year 2000," *Fellowship*, Special Consultation Issue (May, 1965). In addition, he has worked out the

meaning of the concept as one of the themes in the volume: *The Meaning of the 20th Century: The Great Transition.* New York: Harper & Row, Publishers, 1964.

3. Bychowski, Gustav and J. Louise Despert, eds., *Specialized Techniques in Psychotherapy.* New York: Grove Press, Inc., 1958.

4. Callahan, Daniel, ed., *The Secular City Debate.* New York: The Macmillan Company, 1966.

5. Cox, Harvey, *The Secular City.* New York: The Macmillan Company, 1965.

6. De George, Richard T., ed., *Ethics and Society: Original Essays on Contemporary Moral Problems.* New York: Doubleday and Company, Inc., 1966.

7. Dubois, J. Samuel, *The Art of Awareness: A Textbook on General Semantics.* Dubuque, Iowa: William C. Brown, Company, Publishers, 1966.

8. Gibbs, Jack R. and Lorraine M. Gibbs, "Humanistic Elements in Group Growth," in *Challenges of Humanistic Psychology,* ed. James F. T. Bugental. New York: McGraw-Hill Book Company, 1967.

9. Girvetz, Harry K., ed., *Contemporary Moral Issues.* Belmont, California: Wadsworth Publishing Company, Inc., 1963.

10. Gold, Harry and Frank R. Scarpitti, ed., *Combatting Social Problems: Techniques of Intervention.* New York: Holt, Rinehart & Winston, Inc., 1967.

11. Jewkes, John, *Ordeal by Planning.* New York: The Macmillan Company, 1948.

12. Ludwig, Arnold H., *The Importance of Lying.* Springfield, Illinois: Charles C. Thomas, Publisher, 1965.

13. Schoock, Helmut and James W. Wiggins, eds., *Scientism and Values.* New York: Van Nostrand Reinhold Company, 1960.

14. Sorokin, Pitirim A., *The Ways and Power of Love: Types, Factors, and Techniques of Moral Transformation.* Boston: Beacon Press, 1954.

15. Thomas S. Szasz has been concerned for years with the moral issues that arise in such professional areas as psychiatry, clinical psychology, and the counseling professions. His work reflects an excellent example of the fitness of the moral posture in examining

certain social issues in our time. The moral responsibility—or ir-
responsibility—of psychotherapists and the unethical abuses to
which their behavior can lead if it is not morally and socially
subject to critical examination are themes which have been handled
by this writer. In this connection the reader should consult the
following five items by Szasz: 1. *The Ethics of Psychoanlaysis:
The Theory and Method of Autonomous Psychotherapy*. New
York: Basic Books, Inc., Publishers, 1965; 2. *Psychiatric Justice*.
New York: The Macmillan Company, 1965; 3. *The Myth of
Mental Illness: Foundations of a Theory of Personal Conduct*. New
York: Hoeber Medical Books, 1961; 4. "The Psychiatrist as Double
Agent," *Transaction*, 4, No. 10 (October, 1967), 16–24; 5. "The
Mental Health Ethic," in *Ethics and Society*, ed. Richard T. De
George. Dubuque, Iowa: William C. Brown Company, Publishers,
1966.

16. Weschler, Irving R. and Jerome Reisel, *Inside a Sensitivity Training Group*. Los Angeles: University of California Press, 1960.

17. Winthrop, Henry, "The Meaning of Structure and Coordination in Social Planning," *Sociological Inquiry*, Vol. 33 (1963).

18. Winthrop, Henry, "Some Proposals for Experiments in Peaceful
and Non-Competitive Living," *Darshana International*, Vol. 4
(1964).

THE CONTEMPORARY PROBLEM
OF MORAL COMPLEXITY

Editorial Comments

Having moved from Robb's primary emphasis on the individualistic dimensions of man's value concerns to Winthrop's view stressing the social and cultural contexts within which man finds himself, it is very clear that the two treatments are in no respect contradictory. Rather, they represent the two poles of value confrontation with their overlapping territories.

Some social scientists observe that the supposed social given, "the environment," is really not a given at all since it is only an environment *as perceived* by the particular individual in question. Man's mental set, encompassing the cultural values he has already picked up in his society, stands between his actual experience and the "pure" environmental given. Thus we encounter another extremely basic distinction: whether it be stated in gestalt terms (environmental setting plus mental set equals experience), Kantian terms (things in themselves interpreted through the categories of the understanding result in phenomena), or general systems terms (an input transmitted through a program produces an output). Whatever the specific differences in the above models may be, the overall similarities of their three main elements is unmistakable as is the crucial importance of these elements for any understanding of the valuing process.

Four main areas of investigation immediately suggest themselves. First, how do the social institutions that help comprise the "environment" as perceived actually come to be? For instance, how did the draft arrive at its present status in the United States in such a short time? How did apartheid develop to what it is today in South Africa? Second, how do social institutions transmit their value frameworks in terms of mental sets to the people affected by them? For instance, how were various institutions of "the white establishment" in this country able to transmit a "set" to American blacks that resulted in their perceiving straight hair as prettier than kinky hair, thin features as prettier than thick features, and light skin as more attractive than dark skin? And in China, how were the various institutions introduced by Communism able to alter the mental set of many young Chinese from a basic orientation toward the value of the family to one focusing on the value of the State? Third, how can different social institutions be modified and even eliminated? For instance, must the young rebels in the United States actually resort to violence in order to modify the existing political institutions enough to ensure a real "participatory democracy?" And in Czechoslovakia, is it possible for the Czechs gradually and subtly to evolve their institutions far enough to gain the freedom they seek without inviting harsh reprisals from the Russians? Fourth, what are the most effective means for social institutions to alter mental sets? For instance, were the brainwashing techniques used by the North Koreans on some prisoners taken during the Korean War effective on a permanent basis or did the prisoners "backslide" immediately upon their release? And in this country, will the current rash of "T-groups" (sensitivity or encounter groups) produce any lasting change in the participants, or will these groups pass from the scene in a few more years as just one more psychotherapeutic fad?

If man, because of his many potentialities in all sorts of different directions, has a rather wide range of choices open to him as to *what* he should make of himself and his environment, what can serve as the *value* base for his choice? With the awareness of alternatives comes a forced choice for man. He can alter his experience by altering his social environment or by altering his psychological set or by altering both. But what kind of experience is *worth* having? And what can science say in response to this question, having fought so diligently for its clinically detached, coldly analytical, logically objective role that seemingly forbids it making any value judgments?

We will now find Bonner ready to take up the whole question of the *role* of the behavioral sciences.

4

ON THE CHALLENGE TO THE BEHAVIORAL SCIENCES

Scientific Assumptions and Human Values

HUBERT BONNER

European scholars in the human sciences turned their attention to human values only after the cataclysmic events of the First World War. They were warned by the gentle voice of Whitehead to bethink themselves of the false simplicity of reducing human ideals to causally determined events; and Edmund Husserl a decade later laid bare the crisis in European science and its blunting effect on human values.

However, not only did their warnings go unheeded by the behavior scientists but the momentous discoveries of contemporary science and the moral enormities of Hiroshima and Nagasaki did not deflect their determination to construct man in the image of the machine and the rodent, uncluttered by disturbing value preferences. Only the strange and distant voices of humanists and existentialists, of theologians and religionists, whom the behavior scientists either did not hear or help up to ridicule, protested against the blindness to human values and the resulting dehumanization of man.

But the serious concern with values in human conduct cannot await a grave crisis. We must go forward from where we are, however inadequate our base may be. This is so because the problem of values is both the foundation and the apex of human existence. It is no mere academic issue, not simply an act of theory construction. On the contrary, as Ignazio Silone profoundly observed, although we can found a school on a group of theories, on a group of values we can found a culture, a civilization, a new way of living together (9).

Changes in Scientific Thoughtways

Scientific thinking has changed radically since the days of Newton and Darwin. Today it is dominated by the philosophical ideas of Heisenberg, Bohr, and Planck, and by the theories of synthetic evolution and teleological paleontology. Modern physics stresses randomness, indeterminism, and complementarity. Recent genetics and evolution theory hold the view that life is tending in a general direction, namely forward, although they cannot inform us of the specific nature of the forward thrust. Life is conceived as directional because synthetic evolution operates by means of creative natural selection. Like the forward thrust of time into the future, evolution is the elaboration of novelty, the maximization of reality, in which new elements constantly leap into existence. Organic evolution is an exercise of creation on an enormous scale. Judging by the stage it has reached, there can be little doubt that it is moving in the direction of maximum individuation. As every moment of time differs from all others, so evolution, in the long perspective of its onward pulsation, gives rise to an infinite variety of events. Evolution, like human life itself, is the movement of the past thrusting itself into the future, with novelty insinuating itself into the process. In the enormous vastness of time as it moves forward in its unending movement toward the future, man is, indeed, to borrow Dobzhansky's arresting phrase, "the ascending arrow of the great biological synthesis" (4, p. 348).

But modern science differs from its nineteenth century form in several other ways, some of which are necessary to review if I am going to justify my fundamental thesis that the subject of values is a legitimate scientific concern.

The behavioral sciences have over-estimated the value of *opera-*

tionism, even though it was later doubted and partially repudiated by its founders. Operationism, as you know, is the doctrine that only those concepts are scientifically meaningful which can be defined by means of repeatable operations, such as defining length by the use of the meter stick, or intelligence by the use of mental tests. Unless a concept is so defined, the early operationists dogmatically asserted, which is to say that unless everything in science is reduced to rules of procedure, it is not only meaningless but ridiculous. Assertions regarding individual uniqueness or human destiny, for example, fall in the latter category.

With the growing recognition of the subjectivity of human knowledge, thanks to the scientific developments to which I have already alluded, operationism, although it should never be excluded as an ideal in science, no longer holds the dominant position in the natural sciences. This fact opens the door to a more creative conception of the nature of methodology and a more humanistic view of the nature of man. I personally wish to stress what we usually belittle in our narrowly empirical culture, that some aspects of human nature can be described only in the language of metaphor and poetry, in the rhetoric of feeling and artistic imagination. I seriously believe that some things can be fully apprehended only when we think with our feelings.

This statement is neither mysterious nor paradoxical. It means simply that we often feel the truth of something before we fully understand it, because we see it wholly rather than in its separate pieces. I am speaking of that much maligned intuitive grasp of the meaning of something on the wing, while still in the process of becoming. It is the capacity to bear potential, tentative truth, without the need of certainty—or as psychologists now eagerly call it, "tolerance of ambiguity."

The illusion has long persisted in scientific thinking that empirical investigators must rigidly conform to the principle of *parsimony*. This principle, as everyone knows, directs the scientist to avoid complex explanations of natural phenomena and to reduce the number of explanatory concepts to as few as necessary.

As an ideal in the description of many physical events and of simple sensory and differential forms of behavior, the principle of parsimony deserves its honored place in science. However, in its application to the complex problems of personality, the role of values and ideals in character formation, the nature of human creativity, and many others, it either distorts the nature of psychological man or breaks down altogether as a methodological dictum.

There are many human phenomena which can be described and understood only by means of an alternative principle, which I shall call the principle of *plenitude*. This conceptual tool permits us to say boldly that the human personality cannot be delineated in the simplistic form prevalent in contemporary physicalist theories of behavior. Specifically, the principle of plenitude makes room for the subjective life of man, the inner forces which, although not amenable to quantitative measurement and proof, all personal experience affirms to be real.

Among the false assumptions in the behavioral sciences is the doctrine of *reductionism*. This is another manifestation of the principle of parsimony, for one way to simplify is to reduce all phenomena to their smallest units. Thus, thinking can be reduced to sensory processes, personality to the learning process, and moral or religious values solely to rewards or punishments received by a child while sitting on his mother's knees. This reductive simplification closes our eyes to the facts of growth, development, and novelty and propagates the false doctrine that personality, for example, is *nothing but* the sum-total of its separate psychological modalities. The pernicious evil of this bias is that it attempts to reduce every human being to his origin, on the false premises that whatever is prior in origin is fundamental and whatever is first is more important. It is blind to the possibility that man can transcend his past and change himself as he grows toward his future.

Although the great makers of science have either challenged or repudiated the principle of strict *causality and determinism*, most behavior scientists retain it as a basic philosophical dogma. Many distinguished scientists of our time—the creative founders of quantum physics and organismic biology—are no longer hampered by this traditional doctrine. Theirs is a universe in which causality, determinism, and objectivism do not impair the flow of novelty, randomness, and the self-directing character of man. The challenge to outmoded doctrine has come from those individuals who have done most in the creation of the marvel that is science. Erwin Schrodinger informs us that causality is really a primitive rather than an axiomatic idea, and should be discarded. Max Planck's work in quantum physics convinced him that determinism does not describe an event in nature but is a useless assumption. Werner Heisenberg, as a consequence of his important experiments, has come to the conclusion that the existence of an objective nature is an illusion. Biological scientists like Gaylord Simpson and Tehodosius Dobzhansky have argued that as a cultural being man has influenced his own evolution.

These and other advanced scientific views enable the human scientists to argue what genuine human experience has convinced many of them, that as a freely choosing individual, man is an effective collaborator in the making of his own personality.

The foregoing sketch of the doubts and skepticism regarding the foundation and aims of scientific investigation points to what European scientists and philosophers describe as the crisis of contemporary science. This crisis, it should be clear, springs from the disillusionment of some British and European scholars with the ability of traditional science to deal not only with the complexities and implications of its discoveries but with the moral problems of life which these discoveries posed as well.

Those students of science and life who have learned from Whitehead's philosophy of the "turning point" of science can no longer think of science naively as the only source of wisdom. They are convinced that if science is going to save itself from degeneration into a medley of *ad hoc* hypotheses, it must become philosophical and must enter upon a thorough criticism of its foundations (13).

This caveat, coming from an Englishman lecturing in America, was sounded a decade later by a renowned philosopher teaching in Germany. Edmund Husserl, credited with the founding of phenomenology, viewed the conditions as more than a turning point; to him it had the urgency of a crisis (6).

Like so many European scientific and philosophical thinkers after World War I, notably Max Weber and Max Scheler, Husserl was involved in the great debate over the possibility of a value-free social science. After a period of doubt regarding the ability of science to deal with questions of human values, Husserl unequivocally affirmed the necessity of science to concern itself consciously in social and moral issues and to relate those to other vital human concerns. Indeed, he saw in the exclusion of values the source

of the very ills from which science was then suffering: the disease
of positivism.

Husserl entered the fray in the spirit of those European scientists whose aim was to aid, not hinder, science; to advance it, not
to declare a moratorium on it. He wanted to make science at once
more rigorous and humanly relevant. The despairing aftermath of
the First World War made it impossible any longer for sensitive
and original minds like Whitehead's and Husserl's to remain content with a science that closed its doors to the moral realities of
their day.

Thus, the issue of a value-free science is part not only of the
collapse of the value imperatives of daily life and their neglect by
the mechanistic science of our day, but also of the larger issue of
the nature of man in the twentieth century. This larger context,
which is the basis of some of our profoundest philosophies, such as
phenomenology, existentialism, and humanism, was described by
Max Scheler in the 1920's, as man becoming problematic to himself.
He became problematic to himself when he voiced apprehension
over such distinctly human concerns as love, creativity, death, despair, and moral responsibility. These may be called *spiritual* values,
and they describe the unique human being reflecting on his own
being and destiny, on the nature of life and the world, and on the
nature and meaning of man as a form of proactive existence.

Although the narrow empiricists have seen fit to deny these as
data of psychology and the orthodox psychoanalysts have described
them as symptons of neurosis in the same manner as they have described religion, one is blind to the human condition not to see in
man's spiritual malaise the source of his most vexing personal and
social problems. Accordingly, rather than being unscientific for
concerning ourselves with moral values and ethical considerations,
we are unscientific if we think that we can describe the integrated
and healthy person by excluding them.

This concern with human values is no longer exclusively con-
fined to existential thinkers and religious philosophers. In America
the leaders of nuclear science have been in the forefront of a sensitive regard for the social and moral consequences of their own investigations. The horrendous acts of Hiroshima and Nagasaki and
the sobering philosophy of science to which I have already referred
have impelled all of Western scientific thought to become conscious

of the value-related and even personal nature of the scientific enterprise (8). Scientific thinkers now admit what was unthinkable only a short time ago, that scientific objectivity is quite superficial and that the scientists' conclusions are always tentative and subject to revision. And when we look at science in this manner we must conclude with Warren Weaver that the final lesson to be learned from it is that its ultimate and unifying virtues are order, beauty, faith, and love—values which are as old as civilized man himself.

My discussion thus far has established the following reliable conclusion: it is no longer necessary to justify the inclusion of values in a scientific investigation of man. The crisis in Western science and the upheavals in Western civilization in the twentieth century have liberated all but the avowedly positivistic psychologists from the bias of objectivism and the illusion of a value-free science of man.

There is, however, a second reason for the study of values not implied by the foregoing discussion, and this is that values are an intrinsic aspect of human motivation, a fundamental characteristic of healthy human life. I must therefore examine the nature of values, their relation to culture, and their union in the attitude-value complex.

The Attitude-Value Complex

I take it as self-evident that values exist only in an act of choice. Unless one assumes, as I do not, that they exist as inherent "givens," as absolute situations in nature, then values are at once personal preferences or attitudes and cultural norms or imperatives. As personal preferences or attitudes they are deeply rooted in the needs of the individual, in whatever he considers important and holds dear, in what later becomes his style of life. As cultural imperatives they refer to the pressures and norms which, if properly assimilated and internalized, make man's daily life both efficient and satisfying.

Human goals are not only motivated by individual needs but are determined by the value system which serves as a guide to their actualization. Our attitudes toward war, religion, or minority groups presuppose a value system which renders them meaningful. Attitudes as such are only tendencies or potentialities; it is the total value schema of society and the style of life of the individual which make them proactive or future-oriented and hence meaningful.

The intrinsic quality of every attitude is that it is an anticipatory act, a state of readiness or intentionality which determines an individual's relations to objects, persons, and situations in his environment and toward himself as a unique person. Under ideal conditions act and attitude are inseparable and mutually reinforcing, so that an act is what the attitude means, and the attitude means what the act does (2, p. 384).

A value, on the other hand, as we have already indicated, always refers to the interests and concerns of human beings; and hence, any object or condition which acquires interest and meaning for someone is a value. These attitudes and values tend to form a relatively consistent set of acts, real or potential, which I am calling the *attitude-value complex*. It serves as an anchoring point or frame of reference by which an individual's acts and perceptions are organized into a fairly consistent and meaningful experience. Accordingly, when we know a person's attitude-value complex we know *him*.

Furthermore, no attitude-value complex exists in a social vacuum. It is always a product of the culture or the period of history in which it arises, flourishes, and dies. It is at once a tantalizing paradox and a source of human wisdom that insofar as man is universally molded by similar value-orientations, he is very much the same everywhere; but insofar as he individually internalizes the value-schema in accordance with his inner disposition, he is unique.

This paradoxical yet consistent human situation was beautifully stated by Gordon Allport, to whose personal memory I bow my head in sadness. He wrote,

> Each person is an idiom to himself, an apparent violation of the syntax of the species. An idiom develops its own peculiar context, and this context must be understood in order to comprehend the idiom. Yet at the same time, idioms are not entirely lawless and arbitrary; indeed, they can be known for what they are only by comparing them with the syntax of the species (1, p. 19).

Although I do not propose absolutes, I think, nevertheless, that value-orientations approximate universal forms. Florence Kluck-hohn proposed five such value schemata which I shall briefly expound in the following few pages. These schemata bring out clearly the determining effect of the attitude-value complex in the lives of individuals and societies (7, p. 85).

1. *Man's view of human nature.* Man is that being who, unlike any other being, forms attitudes and stereotypes regarding other human beings. In some tribes this goes so far as not recognizing as human beings any others but themselves. Humanness is an attribute which they assign only to members of their own blood groups. In some tribes even members by marriage are not fully accepted, and life is deliberately aggravated for them.

   It is a commonplace that many persons in our society have a low and cynical regard for human nature. The feeling-tone and personality of a person who trusts nobody is quite different from one who, like little Anne Frank, could still, after the terrors of Nazi captivity, say in her diary, "In spite of everything, I still believe that people are really good at heart" (5).

2. *Man's attitude toward nature.* Everywhere in the world men have throughout their history related themselves to the universe in explicit ways. Some look upon nature negatively and with fear, looking upon it as devouring of all life; or with exultation, as something of which they are a part and should enjoy; or as an object to be manipulated by man for his own advantage. The individual who is awed and feels insignificant by the vast and powerful sea differs from the person who feels buoyant as he identifies himself with it. Each of these attitudes, although not mutually exclusive, expresses a feeling of dependency or need, self-confidence or defiance.

3. *Man's relation to others.* This pattern refers to the manner in which human beings establish a community among themselves. Kluckhohn has found three modes of such relationships, which she calls lineal, collateral, and individualistic. In the *lineal* orientation man seeks to achieve his life goals with members of his family, or blood group. In the *collateral* relationship one individual joins with others in attaining the goal of a whole community. In the *individualistic* ori-

entation, which may be either egoistic or otherminded, the person's behavior is characterized as relatedness to others, rather than *togetherness*.

4. *Temporal orientation*. Although philosophers have wrestled with the concept of temporality for centuries, it is only recently that students of human conduct and motivation, excluding phenomenologists and existentialists, have given their attention to it. These orientations, known to everyone, are the past, present, and future. Past-oriented people guide their lives by precedent and tradition; present-oriented persons are primarily motivated by the needs and requirements of the moment; and future-oriented individuals are lured by the challenge and promise of the fore-world, the world which lies largely within their own power to create. They are the proactive, forward-thrusting, self-actualizing persons who are now getting a great deal of attention from humanistic and existentialistic psychologists.

5. *Activity orientation*. Although it is artificial to separate time from being, historically men have placed much more stress upon one than the other. The activity orientations of man have been being, becoming, and doing. Persons who orient their lives around being are basically expressive; they live spontaneously in the moment, as themselves simply and authentically. The becoming orientation, which I prefer to call the being-in-becoming style, places major stress, not on spontaneous being as such, but on unconstrained growth or development, proaction or self-actualization, and to becoming more and more what in his being he has the capacity to become. The *doing* orientation is characterized by energetic activity. "Success and achievement of goals set up by the competitive pecuniary class culture...are powerful motives. The person's goals are much less his own than ends deemed important by others..." (2, pp. 292-93).

I believe that a dependable index of an individual's personality can be constructed from an understanding of the manner in which the foregoing attitude-value complexes function in his behavior. Although there are no formal tests of these orientations, I see no practical obstacles to their construction. Such tests, used along with the Allport-Vernon "A Study of Values," would reveal as much about an individual personality as some of the standardized tests currently used in investigations of personality. As a matter of fact, since the Allport-Vernon test implies some of the orientations, the two might be integrated into a single measuring instrument.

Additional encouragement for this belief in the importance of the attitude-value complex is the work begun a number of years ago and reported by Smith, Bruner, and White (10) about a decade ago. Their study shows that a knowledge of a person's attitudes enables us to make reliable inferences of his value system; and that knowing his value system, which is to say his attitude-value complex, we can obtain a better understanding of the individual. Particularly significant is their report that in a two-hour interview with each of two individuals in the study (Chatwell and Merritt) the question "What things really matter to you most in life?" was the most revealing single factor in the entire repertoire.

Another important fact in this study of the role of the attitude-value complex is that it especially elicited the more creative strategies in the individual's conduct. It is clear to everyone in this audience that many conventional personality tests, especially since they ignore the individual's value-orientation, tend to elicit only the crippling mechanisms, such as sexual conflicts, depressed feelings, reaction formations, and defensive techniques used only *in extremis.* On the other hand, when we elicit from the individual his value-beliefs or his philosophy of living, we bring out his strengths and capacities and above all his creative and productive modes of relating himself to the world.

Many current assessments of personality can lead one to believe that human beings are constantly burdened with self-impairing fears and defenses. On the other hand, tests of what a person believes, how he encounters others in his daily social relationships, and how he feels about people and human events, are basically attitudinal, valuational, and evaluative, and as such give us additional insight into an individual and into our common human nature. An individual's style of thinking about the world, his personal manner of interpreting his and other people's experiences, the nature and intensity of his reactions to the norms of his culture—these and

similar attitude-value complexes are not only reflections of the
total personality of an individual but are also indications of the
expressive and proactive feature of his total style of life.

Although the use of the attitude-value complex in the study of
the human person is open to those dangers which characterize
every vague and highly personal construct and, although individuals
queried on their values and philosophy of life may use evasions and
prettify their disclosures, this is an insufficient argument against
the technique, especially since other forms of personality assessment are subject to the same limitations.

It would illuminate our human nature if I could elaborate a
point at which I have merely hinted by terms such as creativity,
ethical values, and beauty. Generally speaking, psychologists pay
too little attention to the role of beauty and other expressive modes
of thought and feeling. Indeed, the expressive component of an
individual's conduct is a neglected stepchild of most contemporary
psychologies. Yet, a strong case could be made and sufficient evidence could be adduced to show that the aesthetic experience of
beautiful objects, persons, and situations is as humanizing as the
loving encounter, and is an important aspect of it. Paul Weiss, the
philosopher, has especially stressed its creative and ennobling influence on man. He writes:

> The experience of beauty is a crucial experience; to have
> undergone it is to have begun to change one's way. He who
> sees beauty is transformed; under its influence his behavior be-
> comes subtler and more appropriate than it had been before.
> As an effect of it he acts with others more harmoniously than
> he did; he treats things as being more precious, as being of
> greater import, as deserving to be worked over more, to be
> cared for more than they had been. No one can be said to have
> had a vision of true beauty, to have a genuine grasp of a true
> work of art, to have the gift of tongues, to have seen a value
> beyond the reach of those immersed in a given epoch, unless
> he shows in his acts that he is sensitive and concerned with the
> rights and need of others in and of themselves (12).

For reasons of brevity I have also omitted any considerations
of the relation of values to cultural norms. I wish only to say that
although they are not completely separable, except artificially, they

are not identical. Values are more akin to motives as well as to attitudes, for they are based on human wants and desires, and not only on group expectations. Their individual not their social nature is what makes them unique for each person. Attitudes, motives, and values commingle in many ways, and when they are canalized and integrated into relatively coherent forms of conduct, they form a personality. To quote from one of my own publications: "Norms are culturally established categories of action; motives are individual strivings toward desirable objects; attitudes are tendencies to act toward the object; and values are the personal-social impulsions toward approved and desired ends" (2, p. 379).

Summary and Conclusion

It is a regrettable fact that the so-called behavioral sciences, particularly psychology, have excluded the investigation of human values from their domain. This exclusion is no longer justified, for it is based, as I have tried to show, on the mistaken premise that since values are not amenable to objective measurement they are either pseudo-problems or extrascientific phenomena.

However, in view of the radically changed philosophy of science which I have briefly examined in this paper, their exclusion from serious study is an indefensible anachronism. This is the more true in view of the fact that nothing in the whole spectrum of human conduct so embodies and expresses the humanness of human nature as individual and social values. We can no longer adequately study man exclusively in the conceptual framework of learning and homeostatic drives, for this reductionism over-simplifies human behavior, as I have briefly indicated. The learning paradigm so over-simplifies complex human behavior that it completely excludes the uniquely human character of this process. Concepts like reward, reinforcement, and the law of effect, work very well in the description of animal behavior and simple and immature human conduct. However, every individual who has not merely a theory to defend, and who has astutely observed human experience, knows that mature human beings are also motivated by sacrificial conduct. Human beings *give* as well as receive. Indeed, at his most advanced level man is characterized as much by the necessity to renounce and sacrifice as by the need of pleasure and reward. He is moved less by trial and error and homeostatic needs than by the desire to excellence, justice, and honor. Learning results not only from material satisfactions and drive-reduction but also from the need to satisfy our moral conscience. As a matter of fact, as any unbiased observer can see, man often performs acts which are basically uncomfortable and even painful. Accordingly, one is naturally astonished to find that most academic psychologists ignore this simple fact. Any theory of learning that will apply to human beings must go beyond the usual explanations by association, conditioning, and reinforcement, and include what is most characteristic of *human* learning, i.e., rationality, purpose, and value-motivation.

Values are ends to be actualized and fulfilled, not conditions to be ignored and endured. They are important in the study of man because they make for significant differences in human encounters. If this were not so, then man's struggle to actualize his ideals and values would be vastly more perplexing than it is (3).

Viewed in this light, a great tragedy of both modern life and psychology is the disregard of the place of values in each of them. This is paradoxical and disturbing, for the evidence of human history confirms the belief that Western civilization is firmly based on the appreciation of humanistic values, on the belief in the uniqueness of man and the dignity of the individual. An important contribution to human history by Western civilization is its belief in and reverence for the human personality; yet, man's conception of himself is now low and empty. We are, indeed, as T. S. Eliot put it, the hollow men, the stuffed men, leaning together. And, instead of validating his own greatness man's scientific and technological achievements, not to mention his art and literature, have only convinced him of his insignificance. He has learned just enough about so-called deterministic laws to make him feel helpless and hopeless.

Finally, the newer approaches to the study of man—proactive and humanistic in particular—avail themselves not only of the discoveries of empirical psychology, but even more of the seminal ideas of art, philosophy, literature, religion, and cultural history, for an understanding of human conduct. These areas of human creativity can teach us a great deal about man in trying to make sense of his life. In dealing with man in his triumphs, and predicaments, the proactive humanistic psychologist is dealing with concrete and living events, not abstract, unreal, and artificial processes which can be rigorously measured and described by the traditional behavior scientist. His is the only science of man that can meet the challenges of life in our time.

REFERENCES

1. Allport, G. W., *Becoming: Basic Considerations for a Psychology of Personality*. New Haven: Yale University Press, 1955.

2. Bonner, H., *Psychology of Personality*. New York: The Ronald Press Company, 1961.

3. Bonner, H., *On Being Mindful of Man: Essay Toward a Proactive Psychology*. Boston: Houghton Mifflin Company, 1965.

4. Dobzhansky, T., *Mankind Evolving: The Evolution of the Human Species*. New Haven: Yale University Press, 1962.

5. Frank A., *Anne Frank: The Diary of a Young Girl*. Garden City, N. Y.: Doubleday & Company, Inc., 1952.

6. Husserl, E., *Die Krisis der europäischen Wissenschaften und die transzendentale Phänomenologie*, ed. W. Bircmel. The Hague: Martinus Nijhoff, 1954.

7. Kluckhohn, F., "Value Orientations" in *Toward a Unified Theory of Human Behavior*, ed. R. R. Grinker. New York: Basic Books, Inc., Publishers, 1965.

8. Polanyi, M., *Personal Knowledge: Towards a Post-Critical Philosophy*. Chicago: University of Chicago Press, 1958.

9. Silone, I., *The God That Failed*. New York: Harper & Row, Publishers, 1949.

10. Smith, M. B., J. S. Bruner, and R. W. White, *Opinions and Personality*. New York: John Wiley & Sons, Inc., 1956.

11. Weaver, W., "Confessions of a Scientist-Humanist," *Saturday Review* (May 28, 1966).

12. Weiss, P., *Man's Freedom*. New Haven: Yale University Press, 1950.

13. Whitehead, A. N., *Science and the Modern World*. New York: The Macmillan Company, 1926.

SCIENTIFIC ASSUMPTIONS AND HUMAN VALUE

Editorial Comments

After viewing the value issue on both an individual as well as a cultural level with Robb and Winthrop, it is appropriate to delve into the material produced by the behavioral sciences in these different areas. Unfortunately, there is not such a *wealth* of material. There is much more, of course, than there used to be (as Strunk, at least in part, is to illustrate shortly) but nowhere near the amount that the enormity of the various value confrontations of our time would appear to demand.

It seems commonplace to encounter behavioral scientists today who maintain either that they *cannot* scientifically investigate the value issue or that they *should not* or simply that they *will not*. In this article Bonner argues that an enlightened philosophy of science clearly shows that the value issue *can* be investigated in a scientific manner, that the problems besetting contemporary man urgently require that it *should* be investigated, and that any sort of commitment to humanistic values firmly demands that it *must* be investigated. Since much of the controversy over the role of the behavioral sciences with respect to the value issue seems to be based on simple confusion, some logical distinctions appear to be necessary.

First, we need to distinguish clearly between the *facts* that need explaining, and the *theories* that *do* this explaining. Factual statements simply *describe* what *is* while theories attempt to *explain* what *is* in terms of some framework. Bonner has just given the broad outlines of such a framework for the facts concerning human values. A fact may be *about* a value and so may be a theory (though it need not be, of course) but still their functions are quite different. That Sirhan Sirhan attached value to the death of Robert Kennedy may well be a *fact* about a value, but when the question "Why?" arises, clearly a *theory* about a value is being called for. An orthodox Freudian, an Adlerian, a Rogerian, and a Skinnerian could all start out with the same fact as a "given," and yet each might offer entirely different explanations of it in terms of their theoretical frameworks. This brings us to a second distinction.

There are literally millions of questions that can be asked about values, since all individuals have values and all cultures by definition transmit them, but which of these questions is *worth* investigating? Science itself would seem to be neutral on the matter. The methods of science can be applied to any realm of experience in an attempt to find out what facts there are and scientific theories can be constructed in an attempt to explain these facts, but *scientists* are the ones who must choose which realms of experience to investigate. And, of course, what is the basis of this choice except a *value* commitment? Scientists are not automatons who apply various scientific methodologies to problems which just "happen" to be there. The spectres of Paul Oppenheimer and Werner Von Braun haunt many scientists of today: the former, tearfully charging that he and his scientific colleagues had "known sin" for their roles in developing the atomic bombs that annihilated so much human life in Hiroshima and Nagasaki; and the latter, ruefully admitting that he spent more time wondering about how to get his V-2 rockets off the ground than wondering about what would happen to the Londoners they came down upon. If scientists are not haunted by these memories of the past, then some of the confrontations of the present will surely haunt them. The message is plain when viewing the television film clips of recruiters for Dow Chemical being harassed on college campuses by students who condemn Dow chemists for the work done in successfully developing napalm as a weapon to be used in Viet Nam. So, the scientific mill can sometimes grind exceedingly fine in the sense of determining what the facts are and in explaining them, but the scientists themselves must determine on the basis of their own value commitments whether or not to accept the grist offered.

We now come to the need for another distinction. Once scientists accept certain problems for scientific investigation, once they determine what the facts *are* surrounding these problems and formulate theories for explaining these facts, how are they to choose between alternative theories? The answer appears simple. Adopt the theory that is judged best in terms of the objective criteria of science. Certainly a theory that is clearly stated is better than one that is not; a theory that exhibits logical consistency is better than one that does not; and a theory that has been experimentally verified is better than one that has not. But to say that these characteristics determine which theories are "better" than others, and then to define "better" by reference to "objectivity," seems to cloud the issue. Even if a scientist never comes close to investigating values in his role as a scientist and devotes his entire life to investigating only the mating habits of the giant tree sloths in Peru, he nevertheless has *chosen* to eschew the former for the latter and has *chosen* the standards by which he judges his own research, all on the basis of what he *values*.

There remains one more distinction to be made. Once an adequate scientific theory in some area has been formulated, what determines to what use it is to be put? As one might expect by now, the obvious answer is a *value* commitment. After Oppenheimer had been successful in his laboratory, President Truman decided to use the fruits of Oppenheimer's scientific labors in behalf of "the national interest." Fewer American lives would be lost in the long run if the atomic bomb were used, he said, so he used it. And after Von Braun had solved the aerodynamical problems connected with his rockets, it was Adolph Hitler who chose to use this scientific advance to further his goal of "Aryan Supremacy." These two examples clearly show the need for a sophisticated awareness combined with great moral courage on the scientist's part, for the values that determine his choice to do scientific research in the first place may be quite inimical to the values motivating those who have the power to apply the results of his research in whatever direction they choose. And thus the need is shown for a theory *of* value, as well as a theory *about* value. I suspect that it is a mistaking of the former for the latter in the minds of many behavioral scientists that constitutes one of the main stumbling blocks to scientific research into the value issue.

A theory *about* values is clearly *descriptive* and *explanatory* while a theory *of* values is *prescriptive* and *normative*. Philosophers and theologians have traditionally been the ones to enter into the raging controversies over theories *of* value, but they have no exclusive rights on this area. Scientists would certainly be welcomed here, especially since they are usually more concerned with empirical research than with speculation. But at least the philosophers and the theologians have not shrunk from the question of value with such obvious value distinctions as "right" and "wrong," "moral" and "immoral," "good" and "bad," "sinful" and "virtuous," and so forth. All too often parallel concepts are encountered in the behavioral sciences but these turn out to have been smuggled in under other guises: "Mental health," "progress," "well-adjusted personality," "natural state," "self-actualization," "advanced culture," "emotional maturity," "meaningful frame of reference," "creativity," "highly developed civilization" are but a few of these concepts that are sometimes guilty.

So there is a crucial need for theories *of* value, and while scientists can excuse themselves from the task of formulating and advancing such theories as outside of their purview, they need not.

Bonner has definitely opened up a Pandora's Box by analyzing critically the very role of the behavioral sciences, but it was a task that needed to be done. Strunk now performs a similar service in the field of psychology.

5

ON PSYCHOLOGICAL RESEARCH AND EXPERIMENTATION

Personal Values and Self Theory

ORLO STRUNK, JR.

The evidence that the value concept has found its way back into psychological science is manifestly clear. Less than a decade ago Albert and Kluckhohn (2) identified nearly two thousand references on the subject of values. More recently Thomas (79) was able to list approximately eight hundred articles and books on values, most of them appearing after 1945. The 1966 volume of *Psychological Abstracts* records seventy-six references to values, as compared with the eight items indexed in the 1930 volume. Though it would be interesting to trace the vicissitudes of this concept in the history of American psychology, it is not necessary to do this in order to see what has happened to the concept in the period dating from around 1919, when John B. Watson (86) published his *Psychology from the Standpoint of a Behaviorist*, to 1956, when Charles Morris's *Varieties of Human Value* (50) came into the literature. Morris's book, coupled with the appearance in 1931 of the instrument, *Study of Values* (Allport, Vernon, Lindzey, 9) released an avalanche of psychological and sociological research which is only now beginning to take systematic form.

The fact is that the concept of value as an intervening variable nearly disappeared from psychology during the reign of behaviorism. Now—especially since the end of World War II and with the growing acceptance of the mood of existential psychology and even more recently the thrust of humanistic psychology—value has been reinstated as a legitimate concept for psychological research and experimentation.

Yet, there is at present no generally acceptable psychological theory of value, at least not one which provides an interrelated set of hypotheses capable of identifying significant parameters appropriate to empiric testing and, at the same time, rich enough to do justice to values and value schemata.

This paper will attempt to move toward a psychological theory of personal values but in an inflected fashion. The *major* purpose will be to raise the essentially methodological question of how psychologists can hope to measure the dimensions found in value analysis—especially the propriate-peripheral nature of personal values. To illustrate this dilemma, reference will be made to the recently established relationship between religion and ethnic prejudice. However, in using this particular illustration, an introductory suggestion of viewing personal values from the context of self theory will be offered in the belief that it might produce fruitful hypotheses and provide a practical program of research in such areas as education, psychotherapy, and human relations.

Limitations of Present Value Measures

When Dukes (31, pp. 24-50) surveyed the literature on the psychological studies of values over a decade ago, he classified the research into three areas or problems:

1. Measuring the values of groups of individuals and relating the results of other data concerning the groups (individual differences).
2. The origin and development of values within the individual.
3. The influence of an individual's values on his cognitive life.

As part of his concluding remarks of that survey, Dukes wrote, "Psychologists have devised a number of instruments to 'measure' value, though a variety of potentially useful techniques have been largely overlooked. They have assiduously applied these instruments to problems of individual differences, but have, for the most part, neglected the individual" (31, p. 44).

In the past ten years, things have not changed greatly in the assessment of values. Instrumentation for identifying and measuring values consists almost completely of paper and pencil tests (79); and the Allport-Vernon-Lindzey *Study of Values* (9) was, and remains, the primary instrument for examining personal values. While others have critically reviewed the nature and limitations of this instrument (24, pp. 259-73; 30, pp. 597-612; 17), suffice it to say here that the *Study of Values*, though a provenly useful approach for general research purposes, fails to make clear the intensity of value commitments and the idiographic nature of personal value activity. Several other instruments developed within the past five years (e.g., 34, pp. 23-31; 79; 89, pp. 743-51; 41, pp. 483-86; 40) also fail to identify these characteristics.

Despite this lack of sophistication, these instruments are used repeatedly, and much of our psychological knowledge of personal values has its roots in research employing such inventories. Yet there appears to be growing evidence that personal values, like many other similar basically propriate concepts, are indeed *personal* and that their dynamics are considerably more complex than our present psychological instrumentation would seem willing to acknowledge.

Two illustrations might better clarify, or at least point up, the problems to be encountered in any serious attempt to measure personal values. The current research of Gilbert (36, pp. 105-32; 37, pp. 289-96; 38, pp. 69-70) on what he calls "response latency" illustrates well the problems involved in using ordinary paper and pencil tests to measure beliefs, attitudes, and values. The technique has its theoretical roots in German stratification theory (35, pp. 3-19) in the long tradition and research on reaction time (78, pp. 128-49) and in the well known studies having to do with perceptual sensitization (16, pp. 69-77; 58, pp. 148-53; 59, pp. 17-31).

In latency-weighted testing, the subject is presented with meaningful, diagnostically relevant statements, and latency (reaction time) from the moment of presentation to the individual's moving a response lever to the agree or disagree position is measured precisely and electronically. It has been demonstrated that subjects accept a congenial item with faster reaction time than he rejects its uncongenial reversal. In his present research on pretheological students, Gilbert is using items taken from the *Theological School Inventory* (29), a paper and pencil test presently receiving considerable use in seminaries. The instrument purportedly taps seven areas called Acceptance by Others, Intellectual Concern, Self-Fulfillment, Leadership Success, Evangelistic Witness, Social Reform, and Service to Persons. A profile on each theological student is obtained in the ordinary fashion. However, the same subjects then answer the inventory via the response latency technique. Gilbert has discovered wide variations in individual profiles, and upon intensive interviewing it is frequently found that the discrepancies are indeed important to the individual.

In the present context the significant point is that the first "pseudo responses" would have been accepted as valid and reliable data by the naive diagnostician or research worker. The discrepancies, in other words, would be lost in the strictly conscious responses and in the nomothetic framework. Obviously, such a modification in instrumentation can yield invaluable data in such areas as religious attitudes, beliefs, and values (77, pp. 121-24).

A second brief example comes from the recent work of Glenn M. Vernon (85, pp. 156-65) in which he uses Kuhn's technique (43, pp. 68-76) for empirically investigating self attitudes. The instrument used, called *Twenty Statements Test* (TST), is unstructured and is administered simply by asking respondents to provide twenty answers to the question, "Who am I?" Measures of the religious self are then identified by noting the number of descriptions containing religious meanings. This approach Vernon calls the indirect measure of religiosity.

The direct approach involves asking the subject the following questions: How important is religion in your day-to-day living? and How would you rate your feelings toward religion? In this approach, the researcher sensitizes the respondent to the religious area, asking for a direct answer. The assumption is that those who identify themselves religiously on the TST will also produce high measures of religiousness on the direct questions. But, as we might guess, such is not the case. Studies on college students, boy scouts, and various denominational samples reveal considerable discrepancies between the direct and indirect appraisals. Vernon tentatively has interpreted his findings in terms of what he calls public and private religiosity. He then notes that "the nature of the instruments of observation has a great deal to do with the results which are obtained. . . . Careless interpretation could have resulted in quite erroneous and contradictory 'findings' " (85, p. 165).

Religion and Prejudice

That this problem of measuring religiosity and religious values can lead to oversimplifications may be further demonstrated by briefly reviewing the recent research which apparently establishes a relationship between religion and prejudice.

A rather large body of empirical evidence indicates that people holding religious values tend to be more prejudiced than those who do not embrace religious values (5, pp. 9-39; 82, pp. 447-50; 64, pp. 470 89; 1; 44, pp. 103-26; 74; 57, pp. 28-36, 3, pp. 7471-72, 65, pp. 272-75; 8, pp. 1-10; 11, pp. 120-34; 14, pp. 447-57). Allport's tantalizing phrase that religion "makes prejudice and unmakes prejudice" (6, p. 444) raised the question as to what kinds of religious values are being measured, the intensity of the values, or the peculiar *ways* in which religion might be held by the individual. As a result of Allport's statement, a new line of inquiry and instrumentation was initiated. Allport himself suggested the terms extrinsic-intrinsic to characterize the differences—the extrinsic to designate the kind of religion which is a dull habit, something to be *used* but not lived; intrinsic religion referring to religion which is noninstrumental, a unifying orientation of service rather than a manifestation of opportunistic strivings (13, p. 7-21). "Thus," Allport observed, "we cannot speak sensibly of the relation between religion and prejudice without specifying the sort of religion we mean and the role it plays in the personal life" (6, p. 456).

Other workers have come to a similar theoretical explanation, using terms other than the extrinsic-intrinsic designation. Allen (3) speaks of committed and consensual religion. Before the use of the extrinsic-intrinsic designation, Allport (6) spoke of institutionalized and interiorized forms of religion. Vernon (85) speaks of public and private religiosity. And I have used the terms propriate and peripheral religion (76).

To complicate the issue, we now have some evidence to indicate that the religiosity-ethnic prejudice relationship, certainly a recurrent finding in United States research, is not established on a cross-cultural level (70, pp. 419-24; 71, pp. 196-208). Furthermore, despite Rokeach's (63) research on the open and closed mind which leads him to observe that it is not so much *what* people believe that counts but *how* people believe, there is beginning evidence that the content of beliefs and values is an exceedingly important factor in determining behavior (32, pp. 3-13). Spilka (73) notes, too, that religiously prejudiced persons manifest a severe poverty in theological and world outlook, and that this might help account for the relationship often found between religion and prejudice.

Unfortunately the complexity of the dilemma has not as yet been solved because the problem of instrumentation has not been worked out. The Extrinsic Religious Values Scale (ERV), developed by Wilson (87, pp. 286-88) is a paper and pencil test with all those limitations previously mentioned. Though it has been used in recent research by Wilson (87), Allport and Ross (15, pp. 432-43) and others, the recent studies of Tisdale (80, p. 577; 81, pp. 78-84) and Spilka (72, pp. 163-68) pretty well rule it out as a valid instrument for measuring the supposed differences between extrinsic and intrinsic religion and their relationships to ethnic prejudice.

Perhaps one of the greatest values of this excursion into the religion-prejudice relationship is that it has reminded us once again of the complexity of value schemata and the multidimensionality of their dynamics. We are forced again to consider Gardner's question, posed in 1963, "Can values really be measured?" (34, pp. 23-31). He believed they could be measured. Yet the methodological problems, as noted more recently by Wilson & Nye (88) and illustrated here with the example of religion and prejudice, are difficult and challenging, requiring rethinking in the areas of psychological methodology and theory.

Undoubtedly, many new answers will come to us in the years ahead as social scientists permit the value concept to move into their line of vision. In this regard, I should like to mention procedures and theories which might possibly overcome some of the problems of understanding personal values within the context of psychological science. It is realized and appreciated that many other scholars will approach values in different ways, but here I am particularly concerned with noting at least two factors which might assist in the continued development of psychological research in the area of personal values. The first has to do with methodological problems, the second with theoretical propensities.

Liberalization of Methods for Studying Values

Many will recognize in the previous analysis that the issues raised can be seen within those emphases which the late Gordon W. Allport stressed with the members of the science and profession of psychology; namely, the idiographic-nomothetic conflict, the conscious-unconscious continuum, and the propriate-peripheral modalities. Allport first proposed the phrase propriate functions and strivings in 1955 (7), but the term, along with that of functional autonomy (4; 10), did not find a firm place in the psychological jargon. In 1957 I attempted to build the concept of propriate strivings into my redefinition of the psychology of religion (75, p. 138), and later into a perceptual explanation of religious values and behavior (76). I still believe that the distinctions between propriate and peripheral religion can help us to untangle some of the misunderstandings and oversimplifications which have developed in the attempt to arrive at a psychological understanding of personal values, including and especially religious value.

But such an attempt will require a new sort of liberality in methodology—a liberality which will stretch and strain the traditional emphasis of empiric psychology, especially molecular psychology, which by now has demonstrated that it and it alone is not capable of handling complex human experience and behavior (67; 16). Methodological plurality, of course, is very much dependent on the general climate or *Zeitgeist* of a discipline. During the omnipresence of strict behaviorism, for instance, methods of studying values were severely limited. Today, however, the climate is quite different. Indeed, within the past decade a new set of forces has been let loose within the science and profession of psychology. Partly a reaction to behaviorism and psychoanalysis, these forces

are insisting that psychological science is at a crossroad and that as
it maps its future it must place greater stress than it has on the task
of submitting a complete description of what it means to be alive as
a human being (20). This demand, often made under the banner of
"humanistic psychology," is being presented with articulate in-
sistency by such contemporary psychologists as James F. T. Bugental (19, pp. 563–67; 20), Charlotte Buhler (21; 22, pp. 147–74; 23),
Hadley Cantril (25; 26, pp. 13–18), Abraham H. Maslow (45; 46;
47, pp. 279–86), Rollo May (48; 49), Carl Rogers (60, pp. 267–78;
61; 62, pp. 160–67), Joseph R. Royce (66, pp. 11–14; 67; 68; 69,
pp. 21–28), Adrian van Kaam (83; 84), and a growing number of
others.

These scholars are ill content to believe that psychology is only
a "nothing but" discipline; and they are now in the process of dem-
onstrating how a humanistic psychology can contribute toward a
better understanding of human behavior and experience. For the
psychologist interested in studying values, and for the educational
practitioner desiring helpful knowledge from the behavioral sciences, the implications of this growing trend are many and potentially stimulating. As noted, it promises us greater liberality in
methodology—enough perhaps to permit the psychologist to come
closer to the important and essential data of values. And it does so
not on the basis of any tender-minded propensity, but in view of a
growing realization, forced upon all social scientists, that such fields
as value research cannot be approached in the context of simple and
sovereign theories and methods. The behavioristic mechanomorphic
stances simply cannot handle the *facts* of values and their places in
the motivational process. What is worse, the mechanomorphic orientation can, if carried to its limits, distort the human condition
beyond recognition (69).

On the research level this means that we must approach values
with many different methods *at the same time*. Such approaches as
latency-weighted techniques, direct and indirect methods, projective and nonprojective instruments, situational tests, anecdotal ac-
cumulations, personal documents, clinical interviews, and so forth,
must be considered as a legitimate constellation of methods to be
applied to the study of values. It means, too, that the ordinary and
traditional experimental approaches must include phenomenologi-

cal data, a procedure which already has been shown to enrich scientific findings (39, pp. 106-18).

But the climate must be richer still than that produced by this sort of methodological liberality. It must admit also those humanistic approaches and interdisciplinary confrontations which at first might appear anathema to the psychologists dedicated to psychological science in the molecular sense. For it must acknowledge phenomenological data born in a problem-oriented context.

To illustrate this last point I should like to refer briefly to the work of Clark Moustakas (51), especially to his quite remarkable study on loneliness (52). He has called his approach "heuristic research" (53, pp. 101-7), and he places at its core what might be called the existential sources of research. He writes:

> My study of loneliness had no design or purpose, no object or end, and no hypotheses or assumptions. While I was faced with a question or problem (whether or not to agree to major heart surgery which might restore my daughter to health or result in her death) in the beginning, I was not inquiring into the nature or meaning of loneliness and its impact on the individual in modern society. However, the urgency for making this critical decision plunged me into the experience of feeling utterly alone and cut off from human companionship. The entire process of facing the terror and consequences of major heart surgery or an uncertain future and a premature death initiated my search into loneliness. At first, the search was a search into my own self, looking deeply within, trying to discover and be aware, trying to find the right way to proceed, and experiencing a sense of isolation when each path or journey ended with a question mark.
>
> The study was culminated in my readings of published reports on loneliness and lonely experiences. But this was a point near the end, not at the beginning, where it might have acted to predispose and predetermine and color my own growing awareness (53, pp. 101-4).

This kind of heuristic research, coupled with methodological plurality and liberality, might permit the psychologist to come a bit closer to a comprehensive understanding of personal values, both propriate and peripheral, and undoubtedly will lead to greater opportunity in the interdisciplinary dialogue which must come if values are to be taken seriously by scholars in the social sciences and humanities.

The Role of Self Theory

Finally, a psychological approach to personal values must possess some kind of theoretical framework in which to pose problems and offer research programs. Of course, theory is important to all attempts at understanding, even though, as Titchener long ago warned, theories should be carried lightly (28). By this he meant, of course, that one should not rush to their defense or get excited when pet theories are under attack. Yet theories do help us in our research; and in the area of personal values a sound theory can assist in phrasing problems and guiding programs of empirical study.

Here I wish only to note that personal values can be seen as part of that growing psychological edifice called self theory. Briefly stated, in this framework values may be conceptualized as *meanings perceived as related to self* (12, pp. 17-27). In this context, personal values may be viewed as proceptive directions which get their dynamics from their place, or geography in the self esteem itself, or, from another point of view, their place in the ego-world relationships (55, pp. 183-95). Since the research in support of self theory is now well established, it should not be difficult to introduce the value concept into most self schema, whether we are talking about such self theories as those suggested by the perceptual orientation of Combs and Snygg (27); or the psychoanalytical approaches of Freud's (33) later works where the ego began to play a greater role in behavioral processes; or the more elaborate and complex Jungian self system which views values as indices of amounts of energy (42, pp. 1-32); or in the sense in which Joseph Nuttin (54; 56) speaks of ego-world relationships and ego-world unity.

The only point I am making here is that values perceived—or perhaps more accurately, proceived—as meanings related to self could lead to many research designs which would yield valuable understanding of the role of personal values, both propriate and peripheral, in all behavioral areas including education, psychotherapy, and human relations where self theory already has yielded considerable research findings. Within the various self theories we discover a solid recognition of the propriate *and* peripheral dynamics; this should assist us in skirting the failure of much of objective psychology. Also, instrumentation in self theory has made considerable gains in recent years (90), permitting a liberal yet responsible approach to subject matter.

Of course, other theoretical positions ought to find a place for personal values in their motivational explanations. Here I am only suggesting that self theory is in many ways quite compatible to value activities and to recognizing the motivational implications of values in all areas of human behavior and experience.

Summary

In quick summary, I have tried to say that the resurgence of interest in values by psychologists could lead to a better understanding of personal values if, 1) psychologists are willing to acknowledge the fact that paper-and-pencil methods of value assessment are inadequate to arrive at a genuine understanding of personal values—a fact amply demonstrated in the area of the relationship between religion and prejudice; 2) psychologists are able to accept methodological pluralism and liberality and appreciate the power of normative research in order to recognize and deal with all dimensions of personal values; and 3) psychologists are able to place value as a meaningful concept in their various theories of personality, but especially in self theory where personal values may productively be viewed as meanings perceived as related to self.

REFERENCES

1. Adorno, T. W., Else Frenkle-Brunswick, D. J. Levinson, and R. N. Senford, *The Authoritarian Personality*. New York: Harper & Row, Publishers, 1950.

2. Albert, E. M. and C. Kluckhohn, *A Selected Bibliograhy on Values, Ethics, and Esthetics*. New York: The Free Press, 1959.

3. Allen, Russell O., "Religion and Prejudice: An Attempt to Clarify the Pattern of Relationship," *Dissertation Abstracts* (1966), 26.

4. Allport, Gordon W., *Personality: A Psychological Interpretation.* New York: Henry Holt & Co., 1937.

5. Allport, Gordon W. and B. W. Kramer, "Some Roots of Prejudice," *Journal of Psychology* (1946), 22.

6. Allport, Gordon W., *The Nature of Prejudice.* Cambridge: Addison-Wesley Publishing Co., Inc., 1954.

7. Allport, Gordon W., *Becoming: Basic Considerations for a Psychology of Personality.* New Haven: Yale University Press, 1955.

8. Allport, Gordon W., "Religion and Prejudice," *The Crane Review* (1959), 2.

9. Allport, Gordon W., Philip E. Vernon, and Gardner Lindzey, *Study of Values: A Scale for Measuring the Dominant Interests in Personality.* Boston: Houghton Mifflin Company, 1960.

10. Allport, Gordon W., *Pattern and Growth in Personality.* New York: Holt, Rinehart & Winston, Inc., 1961.

11. Allport, Gordon W., "Prejudice: Is It Societal or Personal?" *Journal of Social Issues* (1961), 18.

12. Allport, Gordon W., "Values and Our Youth," in *Studies in Adolescence,* ed. Robert E. Grinder. New York: The Macmillan Company, 1963.

13. Allport, Gordon W., "Mental Health: A Generic Attitude," *Journal of Religion and Health* (1964), 4.

14. Allport, Gordon W., "Religious Context of Prejudice," *Journal for the Scientific Study of Religion* (1966), 5.

15. Allport, Gordon W. and J. M. Ross, "Personal Religious Orientation and Prejudice," *Journal of Personality and Social Psychology* (1967), 5(4).

16. Beg, Moazziz Ali, "A Critique of the Underlying Assumptions, Methodology and Research Techniques Based Upon Molecular Approach to Personality," unpublished manuscript, Aligarh Muslim University, India, 1967.

17. Brogden, H. E., "The Primary Personal Values Measured by the Allport-Vernon Test: A Study," *Psychological Monographs* (1952), 66, No. 348.

18. Bruner, J. S. and L. Postman, "Emotional Selectivity in Perception and Reaction," *Journal of Personality* (1947), 16.

19. Bugental, J. F. T., "Humanistic Psychology: A New Break-Through," *American Psychologist* (1963), 18(9).

20. Bugental, J. F. T., ed., *Challenges of Humanistic Psychology*. New York: McGraw-Hill Book Company, 1967.

21. Buhler, Charlotte, *Der Menschliche Lebenslauf als Psychologisches Problem*. Leipzig: Hirzel, 1933.

22. Buhler, Charlotte, "Considerations About the Role of Values and Beliefs in Human Life," *The Journal of Existential Psychiatry* (1961), 6.

23. Buhler, Charlotte and F. Masarik, eds., *Humanism and the Course of Life: Studies in Goal-Determination*. New York: Springer Publishing Co., Inc., 1967.

24. Cantril, H. and Gordon W. Allport, "Recent Applications of the Study of Values," *Journal of Abnormal and Social Psychology* (1933), 28.

25. Cantril, Hadley, *The "Why" of Man's Experience*. New York: The Macmillan Company, 1957.

26. Cantril, Hadley, "A Fresh Look at the Human Design," in *Challenges of Humanistic Psychology*, ed. James F. T. Bugental. New York: McGraw-Hill Book Company, 1967.

27. Combs, Arthur W. and Donald Snygg, *Individual Behavior: A Perceptual Approach to Behavior*. New York: Harper & Row, Publishers, 1959.

28. Dallenbach, Karl M., "The Place of Theory in Science," in *Controversial Issues in Psychology*, ed. James M. Vanderplas. Boston: Houghton Mifflin Company, 1966.

29. Dittes, James E., *Vocational Guidance of Theological Students: A Manual for the Use of the Theological School Inventory*. Dayton, Ohio: Ministry Studies Board, 1962.

30. Duffy, Elizabeth, "A Critical Review of Investigations Employing the Allport-Vernon Study of Values and Other Tests of Evaluative Attitude," *Psychological Bulletin* (1940), 37.

31. Dukes, W. F., "Psychological Studies of Values," *Psychological Bulletin* (1955), 52(1).

32. Feagin, J. R., "Prejudice and Religious Types: A Focused Study of Southern Fundamentalists," *Journal for the Scientific Study of Religion* (1964), 4.

33. Freud, Sigmund, *The Ego and the Id*. London: Hogarth Press, 1950.

34. Gardner, Eric F., "Can Values Really be Measured?" *Catholic Psychological Record* (1963), 1(2).

35. Gilbert, Albin R., "Recent German Theories of Stratification of Personality," *The Journal of Psychology* (1951), 31.

36. Gilbert, Albin R., "Projective Cross-Examination," *The Journal of Psychology* (1956), 42.

37. Gilbert, Albin R., "Timed Cross-Examination as an Innovation in Personality Assessment," *Proceedings of the West Virginia Academy of Science* (1965), 37.

38. Gilbert, Albin R. and Dana G. Cable, "Diagnostic Value of Reaction Time in Different Formats of Personality Items," *Psychological Reports* (1967), 20.

39. Giorgi, Amedeo, "A Phenomenological Approach to the Problem of Meaning and Serial Learning," *Review of Existential Psychology and Psychiatry* (1967), 7, 106–18.

40. Gordon, Leonard V., *Manual for Survey of Interpersonal Values*. Chicago: Science Research Associates, Inc., 1960.

41. Gruen, Walter, "Composition and Some Correlates of the American Core Culture," *Psychological Reports* (1966), 18(2).

42. Jung, C. G., "On Psychical Energy," in *Contributions to Analytical Psychology*. London: Routledge & Kegan Paul, 1928.

43. Kuhn, M. H. and T. S. McPartland, "An Empirical Investigation of Self Attitudes," *American Sociological Review* (1954), 19.

44. Levinson, D. J., "The Intergroup Relations Workshop: Its Psychological Aims and Effects," *Journal of Psychology* (1954), 38.

45. Maslow, A. H., *Toward a Psychology of Being*. Princeton, N. J.: Van Nostrand Reinhold Company, 1962.

46. Maslow, A. H., *Religions, Values and Peak Experiences*. Columbus: Ohio State University Press, 1964.

47. Maslow, A. H., "Self-Actualization and Beyond," in *Challenges of Humanistic Psychology*, ed. James F. T. Bugental. New York: McGraw-Hill Book Company, 1967.

48. May, Rollo, Ernest Angel, and Henri F. Ellenberger, eds., *Existence: A New Dimension in Psychiatry and Psychology*. New York: Basic Books, Inc., Publishers, 1958.

49. May, Rollo, *Existential Psychology*. New York: Random House, Inc., 1961.

50. Morris, Charles, *Varieties of Human Value*. Chicago: University of Chicago Press, 1956.

51. Moustakas, Clark E., ed., *The Self: Explorations in Personal Growth*. New York: Harper & Row, Publishers, 1956.

52. Moustakas, Clark E., *Loneliness*. Englewood Cliffs, N. J.: Prentice-Hall, Inc., 1961.

53. Moustakas, Clark E., "Heuristic Research," in *Challenges of Humanistic Psychology*, ed. James F. T. Bugental. New York: McGraw-Hill Book Company, 1967.

54. Nuttin, J., *Tache, Reussite et Echec: Theorie de la Conduite Humaine*. Louvain: Publications Universitaires de Louvain, 1953.

55. Nuttin, J., "Personality Dynamics," in *Perspectives in Personality Theory*, eds. Henry P. David and Helmut Von Bracken. New York: Basic Books, Inc., Publishers, 1957.

56. Nuttin, J., *Psychoanalysis and Personality: A Dynamic Theory of Normal Personality*. New York: The New American Library, Inc., 1962.

57. Pettigrew, T. F., "Regional Differences in Anti-Negro Prejudice," *Journal of Abnormal and Social Personality* (1959), 59.

58. Postman, L., J. S. Bruner, and E. McGinnies, "Personal Values as Selective Factors in Perception," *Journal of Abnormal and Social Psychology* (1948), 83.

59. Postman, L., "Perception, Motivation, and Behavior," *Journal of Personality* (1953), 22.

60. Rogers, Carl R., "Person or Science? A Philosophical Question," *American Psychologist* (1955), 10.

61. Rogers, Carl R., *On Becoming A Person: A Therapist's View of Psychotherapy*. Boston: Houghton Mifflin Company, 1961.

62. Rogers, Carl R., "Toward A Modern Approach to Values: The Valuing Process in the Mature Person," *Journal of Abnormal and Social Psychology* (1964), 68(2).

63. Rokeach, Milton, *The Open and Closed Mind*. New York: Basic Books, Inc., Publishers, 1960.

64. Rosenblith, Judy F., "A Replication of 'Some Roots of Prejudice'," *Journal of Abnormal and Social Psychology* (1949), 44.

65. Rosenblum, A. L., "Ethnic Prejudice as Related to Social Class and Religiosity," *Sociology and Social Research* (1958), 43.

66. Royce, Joseph R., "Heretical Thoughts on the Definition of Psychology," *Psychological Reports* (1960), 8.

67. Royce, Joseph R., *The Encapsulated Man: An Interdisciplinary Essay on the Search for Meaning*. New Jersey: Van Nostrand Reinhold Company, 1964.

68. Royce, Joseph R., ed., *Psychology and the Symbol: An Interdisciplinary Symposium*. New York: Random House, Inc., 1965.

69. Royce, Joseph R., "Metaphoric Knowledge and Humanistic Psychology," in *Challenges of Humanistic Psychology*, ed. James F. T. Bugental. New York: McGraw-Hill Book Company, 1967.

70. Siegman, Aron Wolfe, "A Cross-Cultural Investigation of the Relationship Between Religiosity, Ethnic Prejudice, and Authoritarianism," *Psychological Reports* (1962), 11(2).

71. Siegman, Aron Wolfe, "A Cross-Cultural Investigation of the Relationship Between Introversion-Extraversion, Social Attitudes and Antisocial Behavior," *British Journal of Social and Clinical Psychology* (1963), 2.

72. Spilka, Bernard and James F. Reynolds, "Religion and Prejudice: A Factor Analytic Study," *Review of Religious Research* (1965), 6.

73. Spilka, Bernard, "Religion and Prejudice: A Psychosocial Perspective," lecture, Boettcher Center Auditorium, University of Denver, January 10, 1967.

74. Stouffer, S. A., *Communism, Conformity, and Civil Liberties*. Garden City, N. Y.: Doubleday & Company, Inc., 1955.

75. Strunk, Orlo, Jr., "A Redefinition of the Psychology of Religion," *Psychological Reports* (1957), 3.

76. Strunk, Orlo, Jr., *Religion: A Psychological Interpretation*. Nashville: Abingdon Press, 1962.

77. Strunk, Orlo, Jr., "A Methodological Innovation in the Study of Religious Beliefs and Attitudes," *Review of Religious Research* (1966), 7.

78. Teichner, W. H., "Recent Studies of Simple Reaction Time," *Psychological Bulletin* (1954), 51.

79. Thomas, Walter L., *A Comprehensive Bibliography on the Value Concept*. Grand Rapids, Michigan: Project on Student Values, 1967.

80. Tisdale, J. R., "Selected Correlates of Extrinsic Religious Values," *American Psychologist* (1965), 20.

81. Tisdale, J. R., "Selected Correlates of Extrinsic Religious Values," *Review of Religious Research* (1966), 7.

82. Turbeville, G. and R. E. Hyde, "A Selected Sample of Attitudes of Louisiana State University Students Toward the Negro: A Study of Public Opinion," *Social Forces* (1946), 24.

83. van Kaam, Adrian, *Religion and Personality*. New Jersey: Prentice-Hall, Inc., 1965.

84. van Kaam, Adrian, *Existential Foundations of Psychology*. Pittsburgh, Pa.: Duquesne University Press, 1966.

85. Vernon, Glenn M., "Measuring Religion: Two Methods Compared," *Review of Religious Research* (1962), 3(4).

86. Watson, J. B., *Psychology From the Standpoint of a Behaviorist*. Philadelphia, Pa.: J. B. Lippincott Co., 1919.

87. Wilson, W. C., "Extrinsic Religious Values and Prejudice," *Journal of Abnormal and Social Psychology* (1960), 60.

88. Wilson, William J. and F. Ivan Nye, "Some Methodological Problems in the Empirical Study of Values," *Washington State University, College of Agriculture Bulletin*, No. 672 (1966).

89. Wrightsman, Lawrence S., Jr., "Measurement of Philosophies of Human Nature," *Psychological Reports* (1964), 14.

90. Wylie, Ruth C., *The Self Concept: A Critical Survey of Pertinent Research Literature*. Lincoln, Neb.: University of Nebraska Press, 1961.

Editorial Comments

In Strunk's article we find a perfect parallel to Bonner's, for while the latter stressed the need for a critical reappraisal of the behavioral sciences in general, Strunk stresses an identical need for psychology in particular, thus giving us a clear-cut example of how each of the behavioral sciences could initiate such a comprehensive self-study with respect to its own role as a science.

In initiating such a self-study for psychology we find Strunk discussing four of the five value distinctions made in the Editorial Comments to Bonner's article and considered in a general way by Bonner himself. Strunk analyzes the reluctance of psychology, until very recently, to consider the facts about human values as interesting enough from a human standpoint, or legitimate enough from a scientific standpoint, for psychology to consider. In stating the interests of psychologists he touches on their own value commitments as manifested in the swing away from behavioristic psychology to existential psychology and humanistic psychology. Concerning the legitimacy of the value issue as a datum for scientific research, he moves into the area of the psychologists' own value commitments reviewing the standards by which they judge value research, questioning the appropriateness of the testing instruments now used as well as the liberality of the methodological positions underlying the construction of such instruments. He closes by considering the broad parameters with which any adequate psychological theory of values will have to contend. His discussion of such parameters for psychology under the heading of "The Role of Self Theory" also parallels Bonner's discussion of similar parameters for the behavioral sciences in general under the heading of "The Attitude-Value Complex."

Strunk, like Bonner, is concerned here with the scientist's own behavior *qua* scientist. He does not get into the fifth value area denoted in the Editorial Comments following Bonner, where the question of a theory *of* values for determining the use of a theory *about* values is raised. But the relevance of this question for the psychologist as a human being, if not as a scientist, is unmistakable. Henrik Voeward, former Prime Minister of South Africa, was a trained scientist holding a Ph.D. in clinical psychology. Certainly he was acquainted with many theories *about* the valuing process, but what of his own theory *of* values which allowed him to use his knowledge to enforce effectively his policies of apartheid on his country's millions of blacks? One might also consider the moral dilemma of the psychologists in our own country who are engaged in "motivation research" for the Madison-Avenue-type advertising agencies and who attempt to use their theoretical knowledge *about* man to influence him to smoke a certain brand of cigarettes or drink a particular brand of beer. Psychologists, then, at least as human beings, cannot hide behind "the scientific objectivity" of psychology when confronted with this fifth value issue, any more than Oppenheimer and Von Braun, in the final analysis, could hide behind physics.

In the following paper we will find that Banks not only presents insights from a theory *about* values (how both therapists and patients mutually influence each other with respect to their values), but also shows the absolute necessity of developing a theory *of* values to enable the therapist to choose how he wishes to influence his patient; the fact that he *will* influence him already having been determined.

6

ON THE ANATOMY OF VALUE

Changing Values in Psychotherapy

SAMUEL A. BANKS

My professional responsibilities at the Health Center of the University of Florida cause me to be deeply concerned with psychotherapists' and patients' changing values. In seminars with medical and nursing students I try to assist them to examine the behavioral or "lived" philosophies they express in their relationships with patients. A colleague indicated my goals succinctly when he made an interesting word slip on introducing me at a meeting. Describing my work, he said, "That is, this man helps people to have problems." If people are "to have problems" in a creative way, then their values should be a resource which they can know and share.

What is the anatomy of value? The term, like "love," "meaning," and "relationship," is often used but little examined. Let me describe my understanding and use of this word.

Values motivate. That is, they are wellsprings of human behavior. Charles Morris (6) and Florence Kluckhohn (5) have emphasized values that shape cultural and sub-cultural groups. Similarly, individually held values affect individual behavior. Seventeenth century "faculty psychologists" divided man into three

87

parts: cognitive, affective, and conative. They separated in abstraction the decisions, concepts, and emotions interwoven in any human experience. In recent years, students of personality have attempted to overcome this splintered view of man by emphasizing his wholeness of response (thinking-willing-feeling as a unitary process.) Nevertheless, value theorists often divide human values artificially in the same way. It is possible to speak of those affecting feelings and those affecting behavior. From my holistic view, such separation is an artifact. A person's values must shape his perceptions, evoke feelings about his perceptual world, and even affect the conscious and unconscious ways in which he attempts to cope with his perceptions and feelings. I do not simply *have* or *possess* values as I would own a car or house. I *am* my values.

Secondly, values are ubiquitous. There is no area of human experience untouched by our evaluations. Viktor Frankl, imprisoned in a Nazi death camp, experienced three kinds of value: creative, experiential, and attitudinal (2). When he could not find value in life by creating or experiencing the good, the true, or the beautiful, he was thrust back upon another form of valuing. Even in that barren, subhuman world, he could still choose and affirm his own response to pain, indignity, loneliness, and fear. A human being is never without some final expression of value. I would add to Frankl's classification of values one more: nuclear values. By this term, I mean those values behind our everyday values. These are the final hallmarks by which we are able to identify the good for ourselves. They allow us to speak of value, of beauty, good, and evil. The very concept of value implies an ability to identify and share what is valuable or good: *e.g.* beauty, rationality, the quality or quantity of life. These ultimate values are our answer to the question, "Why is anything worthwhile?" One could say that they make the difference between starting the day with the exclamations, "Good morning, God!" and "Good God, morning!"

Finally, values are interrelational. Each value that I hold affects in some way all of the other values that I experience. My values form "constellations" of more or less order. Weisskopf describes some ways in which we may order these value systems by excluding or incorporating new values (7, p. 115). We may build walls between these new arrivals and our old ways of evaluating in order to avoid seeing clearly their relationships. Nevertheless, we are still aware that there *are* relationships between these values, or we would not attempt to separate them. Our wholeness as human beings is affected by the degree to which we allow our valuings to permeate each other.

In the distinctively human endeavor called psychotherapy, valuing is an essential ingredient. For a number of years, therapists attempted to achieve objectivity by excluding their own value systems from the therapy hour. It was considered unscientific to intervene in the patient's valuing or to examine one's own values in the therapy hour. Increasingly, clinicians and researchers are recognizing the impact of therapist's and patient's value changes upon the outcome of psychotherapy.

The patient entering the therapy hour does not check his values at the door. He responds to the interview situation as a microcosm of his larger everyday world. The therapist must understand the values which his patient experiences if he is to share responsibly in a purposive relationship with the patient. I have been in a family therapy relationship with a young man and his parents for one year. Increasingly, I have recognized that I must take into account the particular way in which this son has received the traditional Jewish values about the "good family" and the role of the father in that family. I have difficulty in understanding the family interaction when I ignore either his individual values or the cultural matrix of values to which he responds. Many gaps in patient communications and behavior are filled when we become sensitive to his hidden measures of "better" or "worse."

In addition, therapists cannot and should not exclude their values from the therapy relationship. Marie Jahoda's *Current Concepts of Positive Mental Health* (4) describes in detail the broad spectrum of views concerning the "good life" held by therapists. She reminds us that some groups and individuals stress reality orientation and testing, while others see increasing health as movement toward greater integration of the aspects of one's experience. Still other theories of psychotherapy emphasize adjustment to or adaptation of familial, societal, or other environments. The therapist, in examining his own goals and values, finds that he has already made some commitments regarding the nature of reality, the focus about which personality may be integrated, or the standards or groups to which we may adjust.

In the meeting of therapist and patient, values are shared (if only at a non-verbal or unconscious level) and, perhaps, transformed. Professor Pat Pentony of Australia National University and I developed a Q-sort for the purpose of measuring value changes occuring during psychotherapy. We studied a group of twenty clients at the Counseling Center of the University of Chicago, testing them at numerous points before, during, and after therapy. In addition, we were examining the values of their therapists and of several control groups. Our findings indicate a clinically and statistically significant convergence of patient and therapist values. This is not to say that therapists do or should "teach" values didactically to their patients. It does seem inevitable that values are shared and, in the sharing, affected. Some psychotherapists (e.g., Carl R. Rogers, Carl Whittaker, and John Rosen) have stressed the importance of the therapist's becoming aware of his values and sharing them with the patient, not as a threat but as data for mutual consideration. Whether this is done in systematic, explicit fashion or not, the patient often seems to get the "message." I think of a seven-year-old boy who attempted to order lunch in a restaurant. His mother and sister, without consulting him, informed the waitress that he wanted a hamburger. Ignoring the others, the waitress turned to him and said, "Sir, what did you say you wanted?" He replied, "I'll have a hot dog." The sister intervened, "Yes, a hot dog with mustard for Billy." Again, the waitress turned to the boy, "What did you want on the hot dog, son?" "I'll have catsup, please." As the waitress walked away, the boy turned wide-eyed to his family and offered this verdict, "You know, she thinks I'm real!"

Our current emphasis upon the place of values in psychotherapy offers new risks and opportunities. Let us sample both sides of the ledger.

As therapists turn to the philosophical question of value, there is danger that they may pay less attention to the biological matrix from which human values arise. Gardner Murphy has been helpful in reminding us that values cannot be separated from tissue needs. Abraham Maslow provides us with a hierarchy of organismic drives but indicates that no value can be considered in isolation from the others.

Parenthetically, a number of theologians are making serious attempts to understand various cultural disciplines and sciences. Paul Tillich had more than a passing knowledge of art and of psychotherapy. Reinhold Niebuhr was a recognized authority on political science. As yet, *few have attempted to relate theology or philosophy to the biological sciences.* If man is whole in any sense, we need to examine carefully the relationship between biological needs and human values.

As we consider the values implicit in personality theory, we encounter the temptation to absolutize one value as *the* really meaningful or most significant one. Jahoda offers the healthy warning that a pluralistic view of goals is advisable at this point in the development of psychotherapy (4). We may wish to universalize the issues and solutions of our particular era, lifting them out of their historical context and enthroning them as the ultimate human values. Rollo May has said that something like psychotherapy has always arisen in the periods of transition when old values have become inadequate and new ones are not yet clear. In church history, the confessional, the catechumenate, and the spiritual director emerged as ways of making such transitions. It would be unwise to oversimplify man's complex valuing through an uncritical reductionism that loses sight of man as a historical being.

On the other hand, we must avoid a meaningless relativism by which the importance of the content of particular values is denied. Perhaps, we are too glib in using the word "meaning" today without careful reflection. In man's search for meaning, will any meaning do? Or are some meanings more meaningful than others? One remembers that the Book of Judges in the Old Testament summarized a period of unusual chaos in Hebrew history in these words: "And every man did that which was right in his own eyes."

As therapists become aware of their own values and the effect of these upon patients, a problem arises. How shall he reconcile the poles of permissiveness and intervention in psychotherapy? Is it necessary and helpful to attempt to shape the values of the patient? Are patients' values to alter therapists' goals? Client-centered therapists, Sullivanians, ego psychologists, and other contemporary groups are considering the consequences of their answers to this question.

While there are risks in the examination of men's values through our present approach in psychotherapy, there is also great promise. Charlotte Buhler says pointedly, "We are in the dilemma that, while not knowing any longer what to believe in, mankind feels forever compelled to believe in something" (1, pp. 34–35). As man's ways of believing and knowing are made more understandable, his measure of freedom and effectiveness may increase.

Psychotherapists are making us aware of the relation of unconscious and non-verbal expression of values to conscious and verbal valuings. This growing awareness of the effect unrecognized and unspoken values have upon our daily life is a key to more responsible relationships. Donald Glad's *Operational Values in Psychotherapy* (3) is a case in point. Therapists who understand their own goals are less likely to "bootleg" them irresponsibly to the patient. We must apply Freud's dictum to the therapist's evaluations: "Where id was, let ego be."

Finally, as we come to know our values, we are faced with a crucial choice (literally a crossroads): whether or not we shall *be* our values. They may remain obscure and unowned, or they may be illuminated as we take the risk of revealing the values that we are.

Federico Fellini, in his motion picture, entitled "8½," shocks us with a parable of the effect of our values on others. The movie begins in total silence. You are in the backseat of an automobile, waiting in a long line of cars in a tunnel during the rush hour. The driver in the front seat sits quietly. Slowly, you become aware of a wisp of smoke drifting up from under the dashboard. The driver, in a growing state of panic, realizes that the car is on fire. He attempts unsuccessfully to lower the windows, to open the doors. The camera moves outside the car, and we see the driver battering at the glass with his bare fists. As smoke fills the small space within, we hear the thud of flesh against glass. Now, the camera swings across the surrounding cars. Each person is reacting to the crisis in a different way. Only a few feet distant, a driver is watching impassively, as a researcher would examine a microscopic slide. Two lovers in a nearby car are oblivious to the danger, for their world is limited to their involvement with each other. An elderly couple farther back squirm fretfully, as the husband attacks the traffic jam with continual blasts of his horn. As I watched this man die, I realized that Fellini is offering us a modern parable of the good Samaritan—without a rescuing Samaritan along the way. Even more poignantly, he faces us with the consequences of our values. The values that we *are* become our destiny.

REFERENCES

1. Buhler, Charlotte, *Values in Psychotherapy*. New York: The Free Press, 1962.

2. Frankl, V. E., *From Death Camp to Existentialism*. Boston: Beacon Press, 1959.

3. Glad, Donald, *Operational Values in Psychotherapy*. New York: Oxford University Press, Inc., 1959.

4. Jahoda, M., *Current Concepts of Positive Mental Health*. New York: Basic Books, Inc., Publishers, 1958.

5. Kluckhohn, F. R., "Dominant and Variant Value Orientations," in *Personality In Nature, Society and Culture*, eds. C. Kluckhohn and H. A. Murray. New York: Alfred A. Knopf, Inc., 1953.

6. Morris, C., *Varieties of Human Values*. Chicago: University of Chicago Press, 1956.

7. Weisskopf, W. A., in *New Knowledge in Human Values*, ed. A. H. Maslow. New York: Harper & Row, Publishers, 1959.

CHANGING VALUES IN PSYCHOTHERAPY

Editorial Comments

In Banks' article we encounter a rather different picture of the behavioral scientist. Up to now we have viewed him mainly in his dual role as determiner of what the relevant facts are, and formulator of theories to explain these facts. Now, while psychotherapy does have its theoretical side, its main focus is definitely clinical. Psychotherapists are not attempting just to describe and explain human behavior, but to help their patients *alter* it. The crucial question, of course, is "Alter it in what direction?" Thus, the need for a theory *of* value. Banks opens up this whole value question, both from the standpoint of the patient and from that of the therapist himself.

If we move from relationships in the psychotherapeutic context to other human relationships involving similar dynamics, we see just how many of us must answer this question of direction. Clergymen must answer it with respect to members of their congregations; teachers, with respect to their students; and parents, with respect to their children, to mention only a few. It is a question that cannot be avoided, for we do influence people one way or another. Trying to avoid our responsibility by doing nothing is only an illusion, for doing nothing is still doing *something*. With our theories about values (how cultures transmit them, social institutions embody them, individuals learn them, lives manifest them, and therapists change them) comes power. With power comes the necessity of a choice of how to use it. With this choice comes the demand for some *value* commitment of our own as the basis of the choice. There appear to be three main types of responses to this demand. (We will be speaking of psychotherapists specifically in the discussion that follows, but it should be borne in mind that while the value questions we might raise as a result of Banks' article are of crucial importance for the realm of psychotherapy, their relevance for many other areas of human relationships holds too.)

First, there is the response of the *relativist*. For the psychotherapist who espouses relativism, the role of the psychotherapist is simply to help the patient successfully actualize himself in terms of whatever values he happens to be committed to. If the relativist is consistent in his position, then he is stuck with a world in which service to one's fellow man is no better than exploitation of him, sex with one's beloved no better than sex with anyone who has got the going price, and a commitment to people as important no better than a commitment to things as important.

In our five-fold analysis of the role of value within the scientific context, we observed that most scientists judge the success or failure of scientific theories in terms of certain criteria which constitute their value commitments. Thus, if the relativist in question happens to be a behavioral scientist (as often seems to be the case), what is he to say about his own values as a scientist? Are they not "relative," too? Obviously, not all cultures have valued the ideals of science, and some societies today do not place importance on "scientific objectivity" as we in American society do. Did we not *learn* to value clarity, conciseness, consistency, and confirmation in our theories? Do not our own social institutions *transmit* these values to us? Do not our graduate schools and professional organizations *reinforce* these values in their members? If our relativist really holds to his position and grants that even *these* values are relative, that fact is not "better" than fancy but only "different," we would have to admit that a psychotherapist who espoused such a relativism would seem strange indeed. What justification could he give for *valuing* the helping of people to alter their values?

Practically speaking, what seems to happen with psychotherapists who have a relativist orientation is that they avoid the *reductio ad absurdum* just referred to by being inconsistent in their relativism. They pronounce *relativism* to be an *absolute* fact, never questioning the status of their own subjective criteria for determining what these "absolute" facts are.

Let us now consider the second response that a psychotherapist might make to the demand that he have some value commitment to the direction that therapy should take: the position of the *absolutist*. To paraphrase Banks, some believe that some values are more valuable than others. One holding such an absolutist position does not have to be a tyrant or dictator. Whether he believes that "the good," therapeutically speaking, consists in a patient's developing an adequate set of defense mechanisms to protect his ego, or a patient's altering his ego image and thus not needing defense mechanisms, such a therapist's main focus would be to share this value with his patient, try to convince him rationally of its worth, and attempt to help him realize it. Such a focus is as old as Plato's "philosopher-king" who attempted dialetically to lead his subjects as close to the one true "Vision of the Good" as possible. The absolutist escapes embarrassment, then, over the classic *reductio ad absurdum* used against the relativist: namely, that of attempting to maintain convincingly that value commitments such as Christ's brotherly love, are really no "better" but only different from value commitments such as Hitler's genocide. But, of course, the absolutist has a few problems of his own. First, he must explain the puzzlement over why it is that there are so many "absolute" values but so pathetically little agreement over what they are. And second, he must attempt to justify how he *knows* that *his* absolute is *the* absolute. If his answer to these questions involves his proclamation that he is "the enlightened one," then the relativist will not be the only one who must cope with an embarrassing situation.

Moving on, now, we come to the third response one might make to the value dilemma we have been discussing, a response which incorporates certain elements from each of the other two. This is the position of the *self-determinist*. Between the poles of "any values will do" and "only this value will do" lies the self-determinist position of "any value chosen *in this manner* will do." Thus, the wide range of possible value commitments is retained from the relativist position (though it is not *as* wide as before) and is coupled with the one fixed standard from the absolutist position (though it is now not found in the value itself but in the manner of choosing it). The therapeutic goal is for the patient freely to determine his own values, with three main criteria for judging when the self-determination has been free. First, the patient must be helped in his *awareness* of the situation surrounding his possible value commitments—the givens, the probable consequences, and other relevant factors; second, he must be assisted by the therapist in accepting *responsibility* for whatever commitment he might make; and third, he must be aided in the developing of enough *courage* to go ahead and actually make the commitment in question. Thus some value commitments would not be possible for a patient acting awarely, responsibly, and courageously, but neither would there be just one value commitment open to such a patient. We can see, therefore, the "in-between" nature of the self-determinist's position and as such, of course, how it is open to attack from both sides, relativist and absolutist alike. The absolutist will attack on the ground that there are ways of choosing between alternative commitments even though they were all made by the patient himself in the free manner just described, and the relativist will attack on the grounds that the self-determinist is just showing his ethnocentric prejudice by making his own subjective value commitments to awareness, responsibility, and courage his "absolute" criteria for the evaluation of what he considers to be a free choice.

We see the striking need, then, for behavioral scientists to take some stand on a theory *of* values, before deciding what to do with the knowledge afforded by their theories *about* values. In the following article we will discover that Frankl has developed just such a value theory.

7

ON MAN'S SEARCH FOR MEANING

What is Meant by Meaning?

VIKTOR E. FRANKL

Elsewhere this author has substantiated his contention that self-transcendence is the essence of human existence (4, p. 97). In plain words, being human always means to be directed to something other than oneself. That is, man is characterized by his reaching out for meaning and purpose in his life. And restless is his heart, to couch it in Augustinian terms, unless he has found and fulfilled meaning and purpose in life. This statement epitomizes much of the theory and therapy of neurosis, at least insofar as that type which I have termed noogenic is concerned (5).

However, man's basic meaning-orientation, his original and natural concern with meaning and values, is endangered and threatened by that pervasive reductionism which is prevalent in Western civilization. This reductionism is likely to undermine and erode idealism and enthusiasm, particularly in young people.

Reductionism itself may be reduced by being traced to relativism and subjectivism. Let us, then, ask ourselves whether or not meanings and values are as relative and subjective as some believe them to be. To anticipate our answer to this question, meanings and values are both relative and subjective. However, they are so in a different sense from that in which relativism and subjectivism conceive them.

In which sense, then, is meaning relative? Meaning is relative inasmuch as it is related to a specific person who is entangled in a specific situation. One could say that meaning differs in two respects: first, from man to man, and second, from day to day—indeed, from hour to hour.

To be sure, I, for one, would prefer to speak of uniqueness rather than relativity. Uniqueness, however, holds not only for a situation but also for life as a whole since life after all is a chain of unique situations. Thus, man is unique in terms of both existence and essence. He is unique in that, in the final analysis, he cannot be replaced. And his life is unique in that no one can repeat it.

There is, therefore, no such thing as a universal meaning of life, but only the unique meaning of individual situations (6). However, we must not forget that among these situations there are also situations which have something in common, and consequently there are also meanings which are shared by human beings throughout society and, even more, throughout history. Rather than being related to unique situations, these meanings refer to the human condition. And these meanings are what is understood by values. So that one may define values as those meaning-universals which crystallize in the typical situations a society—humanity—has to face.

By values or meaning-universals man's search for meaning is alleviated inasmuch as, at least in typical situations, he is spared making decisions. But, alas, he has also to pay for this relief and benefit. For, in contrast to the unique meanings pertaining to unique situations, it may well be that two values collide with one another. And, as is well known, value collisions are mirrored in the human psyche in the form of value conflicts, and as such play an important part in the formation of noogenic neurosis.

One may discern and distinguish three chief groups of values. I have classified them in terms of creative, experiential, and attitudinal values (7). This sequence reflects the three principal ways in which man can find meaning in life: first, by what he gives to the world in terms of his creation; second, by what he takes from the world in terms of encounters and experiences; and third, by the stand he takes when faced with a fate which he cannot change.

This is why life never ceases to hold meaning, since even a person who is deprived of both creative and experiential values is still challenged by an opportunity for fulfillment, that is, by the meaning inherent in an upright way of suffering.

By now we have dealt with the question in which sense meanings are relative. Now we have to proceed to the question of whether or not they are subjective. Is it not true that meanings are a matter of interpretation? And doesn't an interpretation always imply a decision?

Obviously, man is giving meanings to things which in themselves are neutral. In the face of this neutrality, reality is like a screen upon which man projects his own wishful thinking, as is the case with Rorschach blots. Meanings, then, would be a mere means of self-expression and therefore something intrinsically subjective.

Actually, however, the only thing which is subjective is the perspective through which we approach the world. But this subjectivity of perspective does not in the least detract from the objectivity of the world itself. Human cognition is not of kaleidoscopic nature. If I look into a kaleidoscope, I do not see anything except that which is inside of the kaleidoscope itself. On the other hand, if I look through a telescope, I see something which is outside of the telescope itself. And if I look at the world, I also see more than, say, the perspective. What is *seen through* the perspective, however subjective the perspective may be, is the objective world. In fact, "seen through" is the literal translation of the Latin word, *perspectum.*

The term "objective" can be substituted by another one which is used by Allers, namely, "trans-subjective" (1, p. 78). This does not make a difference. Nor does it make a difference whether we speak of things or meanings. Both are "trans-subjective." For meanings are found rather than given. If given at all, they are not given in an arbitrary way but rather in the way in which answers are given. That is to say that there is only one answer to each question, the right one; there is only one solution to each problem, the right one; and there is only one meaning to each situation, and this is its true meaning.

Let me invoke what once happened on one of my lecture tours through the United States. Before a question period was started, my audience had been requested to print the questions in block letters. After they had done so, a theologian passed the questions to me but wished me to skip one for, as he said, it was "sheer nonsense." "Someone wishes to know," he said, "how you define 6oo in your theory of existence." But I read the question in a different way: "How do you define GOD in your theory of existence?" Printed in block letters, "GOD" and "6oo" were hard to differentiate, indeed.

Well, was not this an unintentional projective test? After all, the theologian read "6oo," and the neurologist read "GOD." Later on, I used it intentionally by making the facsimile into a slide and showing it to my American students at the University of Vienna. Believe it or not, nine students read "6oo," another nine students read "GOD," and four students undecidedly vacillated between both modes of interpretation.

What I wish to demonstrate is the fact that only one way to read the question was the right one. Only one way to read the question was the way in which it had been asked. And only one way to read the question was the way in which it was meant by him who had asked it. Thus we have arrived at a definition of what meaning is. Meaning is what is meant, be it by a person who asks a question, or by a situation which, too, implies a question and calls for an answer. However it may be, I cannot say, my answer right or wrong, as the British say, my country right or wrong. I must do my best and try hard to find out the true meaning of the question which I am asked.

To be sure, a man is free to answer the questions he is asked by life. But this freedom must not be confounded with arbitrariness. It must be interpreted in terms of responsibility. Man is responsible for giving the *right* answer to a question, for finding the *true* meaning of a situation. And, to repeat it, meaning is something to be found rather than given. Man cannot invent but must discover it. And it is Crumbaugh and Maholick to whom credit is due to have pointed out that finding meaning in a situation has something to do with Gestalt perception (3, p. 43). This assumption is supported by the Gestaltist Wertheimer's following statement: "The situation, seven plus seven equals . . . is a system with a lacuna, a gap. It is possible to fill the gap in various ways. The one completion—fourteen—corresponds to the situation, fits in the gap, and is what is structurally demanded in this system, in this place, with its function in the whole. It does justice to the situation. Other completions, such as fifteen, do not fit. They are not the right ones. We have here the concepts of the demands of the situation, the 'requiredness.' 'Requirements' of such an order are objective qualities" (9).

In his search for meaning man is led and guided by conscience. Conscience could be defined as the intuitive capacity of man to find out, to scent out, as it were, the meaning of a situation, that Gestalt quality which is hidden in the situation. Since this meaning is something unique, it doesn't fall under a general law, and an intuitive capacity such as conscience is the only means to seize hold of meaning Gestalts.

Apart from being intuitive, conscience is creative. Time and again, an individual's conscience commands him to do something which is opposed to what is preached by the society to which the individual belongs—his tribe. Suppose this tribe consists of cannibals. An individual's creative conscience may well find out that, in a given situation, it is more meaningful to spare the life of an enemy than to kill him. This way his conscience may well start a revolution in that the unique meaning becomes a universal value.

The reverse happens today. In an age of crumbling traditions, as is ours, universal values are on the wane. That is why ever more people are caught in a feeling of aimlessness and emptiness or, as I am used to calling it, an existential vacuum (8). However, even if all universal values disappear, life would remain meaningful since the unique meanings would remain untouched by the loss of traditions and the consequent lack of universal values. To be sure, if man is to find meanings in an era without values, he has to be equipped with the full capacity of conscience. In our age it is the foremost task of education to refine this capacity. For in an age in which the Ten Commandments seem to lose their unconditional validity, man must learn more than ever to listen to the ten thousand commandments arising from the ten thousand unique situations of which his life consists. And as to *these* commandments, he is referred to and must rely on his conscience.

True conscience has nothing to do with what I would term "superegotistic pseudomorality." Nor can it be dismissed as a conditioning process. Conscience is a definitely human phenomenon. But we must add that it also is "just" a human phenomenon. It is subject to the human condition in that it is stamped by the finiteness of man. For he is not only guided by conscience in his search for meaning but sometimes misled by it. Unless he is a perfectionist, he also will accept this fallibility of conscience.

It is true, man is free and responsible. But his freedom is finite. Human freedom is not omnipotence. Nor is human wisdom identical with omniscience. And this holds for both cognition and conscience. One never knows whether or not it is the true meaning to which he is committed. And he will not know it even on his deathbed; *ignoramus et ignorabimus*, as Emil Du Bois-Reymond once put it within a different context.

But, if man is not to contradict his own human-ness, he has to obey his conscience, although he is aware of the possibility of error. I would say that the possibility of error does not release him from the necessity of trial. The risk of erring does not excuse him from the task of trying. As Gordon W. Allport puts it, "we can be at one and the same time half-sure and whole-hearted" (2, p. 373).

The possibility that my conscience errs implies the possibility that another's conscience is right. This entails humility and modesty. If I am to search for meaning, I have to be certain that there is a meaning. If, on the other hand, I cannot be certain that I will find it, I must be tolerant. This does not mean that I must share another's belief. But it does mean that I acknowledge another's right to believe in, and obey his own conscience.

As to the psychotherapist, it follows that he must not impose a value on the patient. The patient must be referred to his own conscience. This neutralism would have to be maintained even in the case of Hitler. After all, I am convinced that Hitler would never have become what he was if he had not *suppressed* within himself the voice of conscience in the first place.

It goes without saying that in emergency cases the psychotherapist need not stick to his neutralism. In the face of a suicidal risk it is legitimate to intervene, for it is my contention that only an erroneous conscience will ever command a person to commit suicide. But also apart from this assumption the very Hippocratic oath would compel the doctor to prevent the patient from committing suicide. As for myself, I gladly take the blame for having been directive along the lines of a life-affirming Weltanschauung whenever I had to treat a suicidal patient.

As a rule, however, the psychotherapist will not impose a Welt-anschauung on the patient. The logotherapist is no exception. No logotherapist has claimed that he has the answers. After all, it was not a logotherapist but the serpent who "said to the woman, 'you . . . will be like God who knows good and bad.' "

REFERENCES

1. Allers, Rudolf, "Ontoanalysis: A New Trend in Psychiatry," *Proceedings of the American Catholic Philosophical Association* (1961).

2. Allport, Gordon W., "Psychological Models for Guidance," *Harvard Educational Review*, 32 (1962).

3. Crumbaugh, James C. and Leonard T. Maholick, "The Case for Frankl's 'Will to Meaning,' " *Journal of Existential Psychiatry*, 4 (1963).

4. Frankl, Viktor E., "Self-transcendence as a Human Phenomenon," *Journal of Humanistic Psychology*, 6 (1966).

5. Frankl, Viktor E., *Man's Search for Meaning: An Introduction to Logotherapy*. New York: Washington Square Press, 1963.

6. Frankl, Viktor E., *The Doctor and the Soul: From Psychotherapy to Logotherapy*, 2nd ed. New York: Alfred A. Knopf, Inc., 1965.

7. Frankl, Viktor E., *Psychotherapy and Existentialism: Selected Papers on Logotherapy*. New York: Washington Square Press, 1967.

8. Frankl, Viktor E., *The Will to Meaning: Foundations and Applications of Logotherapy*. New York: The World Publishing Company, 1969.

9. Wertheimer, M., "Some Problems in the Theory of Ethics," in *Documents of Gestalt Psychology*, ed. M. Henlo. Berkeley: University of California Press, 1961.

WHAT IS MEANT BY MEANING?

Editorial Comments

In Viktor Frankl's contribution to the behavioral sciences we encounter an approach that touches on all five of the value dimensions alluded to earlier. First, he values scientific investigation into the whole question of the valuing process. His own commitment to psychiatry is on the basis of the worth and dignity of the individual, regardless of his particular characteristics or circumstances. When one recalls that the context in which Frankl fully developed this commitment was the death camp at Auschwitz, it is difficult indeed not to be moved by it. In short, Frankl *values* man; therefore, he is committed to investigating what man values. Second, he feels that in this investigation he needs to know what the facts *are* surrounding man's values. Third, he has formulated a theoretical framework, logotherapy, to explain man's valuing process which is used by psychiatrists, psychotherapists, and counselors throughout the world. Frankl's theory is counterposed to Freud's and Adler's; based not on the will to pleasure or the will to power, but on "the will to meaning." Fourth, in evaluating the worth of these alternative theories, we find Frankl committed to various *value standards* which function as criteria of judgment for the theories. Obviously, he feels that other theorists have been too narrow in their formulations, viewing man as too much of a bare psychological mechanism and thereby leaving out certain uniquely human elements. Fifth, his own stance as a psychotherapist very clearly reveals his own theory *of* values.

In Frankl's view of the direction in which therapy should move, we find an example of the self-determinist's position. For Frankl, the relativist's position is to be denied. People whose value commitments condemn them to living in "the existential vacuum" (the "Mr. Joneses" of contemporary folk music) are not just *different* from those whose value commitments allow them to live a life of meaning (the "beautiful people") but also, unfortunately, are immature. The absolutist's position is to be denied, too. The logotherapist is the least tempted of all psychotherapists to impose value judgments on the patient. Instead, Frankl has originated a type of therapy in which the patient is first made aware, then made responsible, and finally made courageous, all so that he might truly and freely be himself. The patient becomes aware that a "will to meaning" is basic to the human situation; aware that man is much more than a mere mechanism; and aware that many of man's problems can be noogenically traced to either a lack of meaning in his life or a conflict of different meanings in his life. He will be *responsible* in the sense that he sees that man has the ability to make himself and refuses to hand over this task to the therapist or anyone else. And he becomes *courageous* in that he responds affirmatively to the demand which requires him to live his life according to his conscience, never knowing whether or not it has been "the true meaning" to which he has been committed.

In answer, then, to Bank's dilemma over the influence of the therapist on the values of his patient, Frankl answers boldly that it is the therapist's role to dedicate himself to helping his patient *search* for some value that will give meaning to his life, but with the full realization and acceptance that the patient must ultimately *find* this value for himself.

As Douglas, in the following article, examines the religious dimensions of value, he presents, like Frankl, not only a psychological theory *about* values but key concepts from a theory *of* value as well.

8

ON THE COMPONENTS OF FAITH

Faith as a Factor in Value Motivation

WILLIAM DOUGLAS

A basic problem related to the understanding of value motivation is: the nature and function of faith as psychic process. As a psychologist, my preferred term would be faith, as that of a sociologist would be religion.

Let us look in particular at four components of a faith: awe, trust, obedience, and meaning. (As a memory device, it will be noted that the first letters of awe, trust, obedience, and meaning spell "ATOM," and these components are in a sense the "molecules" which in complex interaction produce the "atom" of faith.) To analyze a person's faith means to describe the nature, the strength, and the function of each of the components in complex interaction with one another. A concrete instance of faith might be represented by an equation with different loadings of these four components, plus other components unique to the person. In equation form:

$$\text{Faith} = f \ (A \times T \times O \times M \dots Y \times Z) \text{ with Y and Z representing factors particular to this case.}$$

To begin with *awe*, Huston Smith, like Carl Jung, considers this to be the most basic and universal element in religious experience. Awe, as William James put it, involves recognition of a primal reality to which the appropriate response is neither a curse nor a jest. There is an "Idea of the Holy" (5) as the numinosum, a mysterious, tremendous Other, which is both fascinating and frightening. In stimulus-response terms, it may be this combination of attraction (approach gradient) and repulsion (avoidance gradient) which produces anxiety regarding the Holy. Or, in more homely terms, people are motivated to attend church, but also motivated to sit toward the back. To speculate further, this time in Freudian terms, awe leads to anxiety which leads to repression, especially of strong positive and negative affect.

In any event, the first component of faith is awe: a state more difficult perhaps to attain in "the secular city." In our time and place, sacred-profane distinctions are obliterated, or more precisely, the profane is glorified, as we say in public what we might be ashamed to think in private. Awe is more difficult to experience in a period in which a boy looks into the heavens and asks his father—in this case William Hamilton—"Which ones did *we* put there, daddy?" (Incidentally, in the age of the "new morality" of the "situational ethic," Kant's reliance on the moral law within is subject to as much attack as his assumption of reverence before the starry sky above.) Awe requires awareness of the transcendent, of a reality which persists in the midst of decay, defeat, death, and unrequited desire. It was this awareness which led Gautama, the Buddha, into the search for enlightenment, and Teresa of Avila into the mystic way.

If awe is awareness of the transcendent, *trust* is awareness of the imminent. At Easter, Christians celebrate in awe the transcendent victory over evil and death. At Christmas, Christians celebrate in trust the entrance into history of "God-with-us" in the most unlikely form and setting. Trust is the dominant component in the "good old hymns" of the nineteenth century: God will take care of me; I need Thee every hour; He leadeth me; Just as I am, without one plea; Help of the helpless, O abide with me. This component is stressed also in the inspirational literature summarized by Schneider and Dornbusch in their survey of *Popular Religion* (6). Indeed, in the general usage of the word faith, it is this component of trust which is most stressed. It was this partial, and often self-serving, version of faith that Freud attacked in his *Future of an Illusion* (4).

Trust is a valid and necessary component of faith, but like all other components, it can be distorted into demonic and/or idolatrous expressions. This is true also of obedience. Indeed, the free, loving obedience of a son is so often distorted into the rigid, moralistic, self-righteous obedience of an elder brother who judges the disobedient ("we missed you!") that the term tends to have negative connotations. If you prefer, substitute loyalty for obedience. But, in any event, obedience (or loyalty) is the conative or *behavioral* component of faith, as awe and trust are the *affective* components, dealing with the transcendence and immanence of what an individual holds central in existence. Awe and trust are *feelings* (or, if you prefer, states of existence) in relation to what a person considers ultimate or central. Obedience is a matter of loyalty to a standard, which may be expressed in a person. "Trust and obey, there is no other way," goes the hymn. And, in a different theological context, Paul Tillich interprets faith as involving both the unconditional promise of the Covenant's "I will be your God" and the unconditional demand of the Covenant's "And you shall be my people." The appropriate response to the promise is trust, and to the demand, obedience. It is significant, at this point, that in the Old Testament, the question God most frequently asks of man is not "Who are you?"—the identity issue of our time—but rather: "What are you *doing* here?"

As I have indicated, both trust and obedience can be, and often are, distorted. Over-emphasis on the wrong form of trust, without corresponding emphasis on obedience, can lead to conformist, shallow, extrinsic faith. Over-emphasis on the wrong form of obedience, without corresponding emphasis on trust, can lead to either Pharisaism or guilt-ridden self-condemnation. There is Law, but there is also Gospel, discipline but also freedom. Moreover, the nature of a person's obedience is likely to be related to the nature of his trust. Thus, in his discussion of a "schedule of virtues" in *Insight and Responsibility* (3), Erik Erikson refers to fidelity, the key virtue of adolescence, as depending on "the rudiments of virtue developed in childhood": hope, will, purpose, and competence. For you cannot be truly loyal until you have learned to hope, on the basis of trust. In addition, fidelity requires the exercise of free choice, in terms of valued goals, using all of one's powers in the completion of tasks undertaken. Fidelity depends, then, on hope, expressed in will, shaped by purpose, and disciplined into competence. To put it in the classic phrase of Earl Loomis, the eunuch cannot sacrifice his virginity. Only with disciplined, goal-directed freedom, as well as trusting hope, is true fidelity or loyal obedience possible. Only then is the yoke (same root as yoga—both referring to discipline) a mark of service rather than servitude. And, as Erikson points out, as the adolescent virtue of fidelity depends on the childhood virtues of hope, will, purpose, and competence, so do the adult virtues of love, care, and purpose depend in turn on fidelity.

Faith includes, then, the *affective* components of awe and trust, and the *behavioral* component of obedience. In addition, there is a *cognitive* component to faith: *meaning*. For, faith involves not only feelings and actions, but also thoughts, as these structure a "unifying philosophy of life." If awe, trust, and obedience relate to the way in which we relate to what we consider ultimate, meaning has to do with the *nature* (or "contents") of the *object* of relationship. To quote Gordon Allport in his discussion of the mature religious sentiment (1, *The Individual and His Religion*, p. 57) the meaning component refers to "conceptual objects and principles that the individual regards as of ultimate importance in his own life, and as having to do with what he regards as permanent or central in the nature of things." Meaning, in Kurt Lewin's terms, relates to the differentiation and integration of a person's life space. In Allport's model of personality development, the meaning component relates to the proprium (1, *Becoming* and *Pattern and Growth in Personality*) which includes factors such as sense of bodily self, self-identity, self-esteem, extension of self, social self-image, rational coping, and propriate striving.

Clarification of the meaning component also comes from Jerome Bruner (2). Bruner sees growth as a process of transforming experiences representationally into cognitive (orienting and organizing) models through three levels of learning. The first level, the *enactive*, involves the acquisition through *action* of an appropriate set of responses and habit patterns—cf. the obedience component of faith. The second level, the *ikonic*, is governed by summary images and perceptual organization through *imagination*, in which images awaken and orient the person to his environment. (Cf. the *awe* and *trust* components, with summary images such as Creator and Redeemer, Father and Son, Samaritan and Shepherd, Pharisee and Publican, Cross and Manger.) The third level, the *symbolic*, involves the translation of experience into language, using logical propositions at the abstract level of working models. Language, as an instrument of thinking, frees the person from determination by present stimuli, and allows him to conserve past experience in organized ways. Likewise, language allows the person to use his understanding to move from the familiar and known into the unfamiliar and unknown. (Cf. Harry Stack Sullivan's concepts of the prototaxic, parataxic, and syntaxic.) Faith, in Bruner's conceptual model, involves, then, the enactive (obedience), ikonic (awe and trust), and symbolic (meaning) levels—developed in that order in normal personality development.

Such a model of development and of faith clearly involves value motivation, and not simply drive motivation, need motivation, or tension-reduction motivation. I am assuming a model of self-actualization with constituent concepts such as propriate striving and the functional autonomy of motives. With Allport, I am regarding motives (at least for the healthy adult) as varied, self-sustaining, contemporary systems, and not simply as sublimated forms of basic, biologically-grounded drives seeking the increase of pleasure and the reduction of pain. I am assuming an existentialist, rather than a Freudian or stimulus-response or behaviorist model. I recognize, in Max Planck's words, that "a scientist can be a scientist for only a few minutes, and then he becomes a metaphysician."

For, if behavioral science is to be concerned with prediction and control, as well as understanding, then goals and values will necessarily be involved, and the question of the nature of man—which Allport said is the most crucial issue in all psychological theory—will be raised. Control or guidance implies, in Seward Hiltner's words, some sort of "otherness" which functions through consultation or imposition. But what *kind* of otherness? Does it function in the best interests of human welfare? And here, clearly, my assumptions differ from those of B. F. Skinner, as expressed in *Walden Two* (7):

> We can achieve a sort of control under which the con-
> trolled, though they are following a code much more
> scrupulously than was ever the case under the old system,
> nevertheless *feel free*. . . . there's no restraint and no revolt.
> By a careful cultural design, we control not the final be-
> havior, but the *inclination* to behave—the motives, the de-
> sires, the wishes. . . . What is love except another name for
> the use of positive reinforcement?

Yet, in Skinner's account of what he would regard as a Utopian society (and I gather that his views on these issues have changed little since the book's publication almost twenty years ago) one must ask: What are the values shaping the cultural design? And to me, at least, they appear to be the old homely virtues, probably those of Skinner's parents, of thrift, efficiency, cooperation, and the dignity of labor.

While, as a former Eagle Scout and, more important, son of Scottish immigrant parents, I would have little objection to these values, I do object to the "father knows best" imposition of them on the controlled by the wise, benevolent managers of *Walden Two*. For me, and here I am in the existentialist, humanist tradition, a central value is that of the conception of man as a free, conscious, responsible, being-in-the-world. I choose to believe in not only self-actualization but also self-transcendence. I prefer a model of human nature which considers personality as expanding, growing, creating—aware of possibilities and therefore open to decision— faced, as Kierkegaard put it, with the "awful possibility of being able." For, I agree with Heidegger, that man lives not only in the Umwelt which Skinner stresses, but also in the modes of Mitwelt and Eigenwelt.

What I am seeking to express is the meaning component of my faith: "conceptual objects and principles that the individual regards as of ultimate importance in his own life, and as having to do with what he regards as permanent or central in the nature of things." Only someone who accepts most of the propositions I have just stated concerning the nature of man is likely to accept the model of faith which I have presented. Not even all who call themselves existentialists or humanists would accept my conceptual objects and principles in the exact form I have communicated them. The phenomenology of faith presented in this paper is, therefore, inevitably testimony as much as description, consisting of what Collingwood called "interprefacts." Nevertheless, I would still maintain that the distinctions I have been seeking to draw among the various components of faith, and the description of their interactions and potential distortions, have both theoretical and practical usefulness.

To describe faith as a psychic process is clearly no easy task. But the component model I have presented may be one step toward that end. At least, I hope so. Perhaps, in the future, we may be more precise in our communication, and more aware of some of the sources of our disagreements. And this can be the beginning of wisdom.

REFERENCES

1. Allport, Gordon W., *The Individual and His Religion.* New York: The Macmillan Company, 1950. *Becoming,* New Haven: Yale University Press, 1955. *Pattern and Growth in Personality.* New York: Holt, Rinehart & Winston, Inc., 1961.

2. Bruner, Jerome, *On Knowing.* Cambridge: Harvard University Press, 1962. *The Process of Education.* Cambridge: Harvard University Press, 1963. *Toward a Theory of Instruction.* Cambridge: Harvard University Press, 1966.

3. Erikson, Erik, *Insight and Responsibility.* New York: W. W. Norton & Company, Inc., 1964.

4. Freud, Sigmund, *Future of an Illusion.* New York: Anchor Books, Doubleday & Company, Inc., 1961.

5. Otto, Rudolph, *The Idea of the Holy.* London: Oxford University Press, 1943.

6. Schneider, Louis and S. Dornbusch, *Popular Religion.* Chicago: University of Chicago Press, 1958.

7. Skinner, B. F., *Walden Two.* New York: The Macmillan Company, 1962.

Editorial Comments

The next step in our logical progression finds us with an example of an investigation into one of the key items that any general analysis of the value issue must touch on, faith as a factor in value motivation. We also find this investigation coming as a result of the type of enlightened scientific viewpoint that Bonner is attempting to promote, and illustrating how attempts can be made to overcome some of the methodological problems of psychology as a particular science that Strunk brings up. In addition, there is a model of the self which is discussed as part of a tentative theory *about* value; in the criticizing of certain emphases in faith states, a theory *of* value is in evidence.

We find Douglas tackling one of the most significant and certainly one of the thorniest of theological issues, faith states. But instead of discussing these states at a strictly theological level he attempts to analyze logically their different component parts, in order to move in the direction of tying down these components empirically to actual experience amenable to scientific investigation. Thus, instead of staying within the realm of theology in discussing his four basic components of faith (awe, trust, obedience, and meaning) he brings in the psychological categories of affective response, behavioral response, and cognitive response as basic theoretical concepts. And since people in faith states think, feel, and act, and since all of these components are fundamental aspects of human experience, they constitute legitimate data (facts about values) for psychological study. For instance, when Douglas observes that the component of awe can be approached via the stimulus-response concepts of approach gradient and avoidance gradient we are, perhaps, in the initial phase of an operational definition for this facet of experience.

In addition to attempting to develop an appropriate method for description of the facts concerning the various components of faith states as they relate to value motivation, Douglas also observes that he is "assuming a model of self-actualization with constituent concepts such as propriate striving and the functional autonomy of motives," which clearly is inviting a theory *about* these facts. Finally, he also refers to a theory of value in critically evaluating some of the faith components of value which he has already described and explained, as is shown in his reference to the distortion of some of the components: their over-emphasis, shallowness, and incorrect form.

If trained psychologists such as Douglas were to run behavioral studies on the various components of the faith experiences of the orthodox believers in their middle-class suburban churches as contrasted with those of some of the "God is Dead-New Morality" believers in their underground churches, perhaps some light rather than heat would be shed on this current area of confrontation. Psychology obviously would have a very important role to play in the clarification and hopeful solution of such conflicts.

Now we turn to an analysis by Foster of the concept of value from different views of religious experience.

9

ON MODELS FOR MAN

Valuing as Religious Experience

ARTHUR L. FOSTER

Where a thinker finally arrives in his theory of man, and hence in his understanding of values, depends upon the model he adopts for comprehending man. Here is one such "root metaphor" as formulated by an engineer in a large American company:

> Man is a complete, self-contained, totally enclosed power plant, available in a variety of sizes, and reproducible in quantity. He is relatively long-lived, has made major strides toward solving the spare parts problem. He is water-proof, amphibious, operates on a wide variety of fuels; enjoys thermostatically-controlled temperature, circulating fluid heat, evaporative cooling; has sealed, lubricated bearings, audio and optional direction and range finders, sound and sight recording, audio and visual communication, and is equipped with an automatic control called a brain (6, p. 29).

Once one has accepted the adequacy of a machine analogy, then his theory of human valuing is also set. Gordon Allport in his various writings has shown the value consequences which flow from the adoption of machine, animal, child, or pathological models as our starting point (1, *Personality and Social Encounter*, pp. 55-109; *Becoming*, pp. 1-19, 99-101). Recognition of the crucial significance of the primary metaphor has led European existential psychiatrists to insist that the "only model for man is man" (2, pp. 191-213). This, if I understand correctly, is the thesis of Ludwig Binswanger. Here in America Abraham Maslow is proposing a variation on this very theme, namely, that we take as our beginning point the human being at his peak experiencing, in the fullness of self-actualization and self-transcendence.

Finally, we must recognize that theologians take still another starting point. We say "the ultimate model for man is God." Man is made in the image of God and any view of man that omits, denies, or overlooks that value relation seems to us to be a falsifying of human nature. But now we must move from a consideration of the variety of primary models for viewing man and valuing to the question of the meaning of valuing.

What is valuing? Is it the process of discovering the *intrinsic* goodness, beauty, or truth of an object? Is it a *bestowing* of value on that which is valueless in and by itself? Is it a *relation* of subject and object, such that value appears as the quality of that relationship? Or finally is valuing a contextual act, a situational meaning deriving not only from the relation of subject and object but of all operating physical, biological, personal, social, economic, and political forces? How one answers these questions depends upon his philosophical standpoint. A naive realist will locate value in the thing itself. The idealist will attribute value to the appreciative consciousness of the self. Buber finds the focus of valuing to be in the "betweenness" of persons, and ultimately in God. Whitehead conceives of value as inseparably linked with *being*, so that every event, every relation, and every interpersonal situation is value-laden, and God in his "primordial nature" defines the range of possible valuings, while God in his "consequent nature" conserves the values of the universe.

Our proposal is that some such relational and/or contextual theory is essential to do justice to the complexities involved in the process of valuing. Facts and values, reality and purpose, persons and meaning, must always be perceived as inextricably bound together. It seems to me, then, a curious irony that psychology—the science of the psyche—should have devoted so much of its energy in the past one hundred years to a taboo on valuing—*to the value of banishing value* from our conceptions of man and from our research methodology. Yet, it has remained for the psychotherapists to become heralds of the rebirth of the creative, initiating, valuing self. Also they have discerned how profoundly the valuings of the healer influence the patient (and vice versa) and how fundamentally the doctor's research reflects his value perspectives. Objectivity, in research, then becomes an awareness of one's own valuings rather than a presumed absence of such commitments.

Such a conception of man as a valuing being opens the door for newer conceptions of health and illness. Instead of conceiving psychological sickness as chiefly the result of repression of the id by the introjected tyrannical superego values, it becomes possible also to see man's malaise in terms of value conflicts or of value emptiness. Man can be viewed as suffering not only from unwarranted guilt feelings, but from the real guilt of the violation of authentic values. The way is cleared for conversation of psychology with theology, and with the psychology and phenomenology of religion.

One of the most profound analysts of religious experience was Rudolph Otto (4). Out of his studies in the history of religions and his own existential involvement in the Hebraic-Christian stream, Otto arrived at his view of the Holy. Deeper than one's perception of the beautiful, the morally good, or the rational is, Otto holds, an experienceable relation of the self with "the wholly other." One meets ultimate mystery, which at once fascinates and fills the self with awe and dread. It is a transforming moment of self-recognition in that one becomes aware of his true condition and significance in relation with the really real. So Isaiah cried out "Woe is me for I am a man of unclean lips." Central to this experience of the Holy is the matter of valuing. This valuing is, like most of man's valuing, carried on at an intuitive, non-rational level of feeling. Yet feeling, for Otto as for Whitehead, is a vital method of knowing and valuing, and is not to be confused with mere emotion.

Another approach to the dimension of valuing in religious experience is that of Paul Tillich (5, pp. 11-15). A man's real religion and his real god is his ultimate concern. Thus a man may be committed at the conscious explicit level to the God of Christianity, Judaism, or Islam; yet at the implicit unconscious operational level his real loyalty may be given for example, to the value of status-seeking. Or a man may be a conscious atheist and yet be giving unreserved loyalty, at a depth level, to some personal or social value such as truth. This is his operational god. This is his existential absolute. This is his religious commitment—which integrates and unites his life.

Tillich's concept of ultimate concern also allows one to carry out an analysis of idolatry. Idolatry is commitment of oneself totally to what is not of ultimate value. It is to treat a proximate or partial good as though it were of ultimate worth. On this basis one can understand all of life as inescapably religious. Healthy personality development, for example, involves carrying out tasks and commitments appropriate to the self at that time and place. But if one refuses to let the old integration die then no new one can be born. The self is then in the idolatry of making a part into the whole.

Religious experience, thus conceived, is not monolithically good. For idolatry is a kind of religious experience also—and it is inescapably a human experience—whether a man is formally religious or not. In the same manner, the divided self or the conflicted self can be conceived as polytheistic. Values may have negative as well as positive power in the psyche! They work to integrate or to disintegrate the self. Or they may be functionally and temporarily integrative of the self but unworthy objects of its ultimate concern! Like all ideals a false god delivers—really delivers—for a time. But it leads us to final disillusionment and destruction.

Using Tillich's model for understanding religious experience, then, it becomes clear that the psychotherapeutic process can be conceived as a search for values—not only for *proximate* but *ultimate concerns*. It may be conceived as a search for reality. It is a prophetic process of exposure of one's idolatries and of one's polytheisms. Erich Fromm's psychology of religion, derived from his clinical and cultural studies, makes the same point in his discussion of the private religions of the developing self, as well as in his contention that possession of a frame of reference and object of devotion is a universally human characteristic (3).

In summary, we have attempted to do three things. First we tried to show the importance for the valuing process of taking the conception of man as made in the image of God. Secondly, we explored several alternative theories of valuing. Finally, we have shown how two influential modern thinkers have understood valuing as religious experience.

REFERENCES

1. Allport, Gordon, *Personality and Social Encounter*. Boston: Beacon Press, 1960. *Becoming*. New Haven: Yale University Press, 1955.

2. Binswanger, Ludwig, "The Existential Analysis School of Thought," in *Existence*, eds. Rollo May, Ernest Angel, and Henri F. Ellenberger. New York: Basic Books, Inc., Publishers, 1958.

3. Fromm, Erich, *Psychoanalysis and Religion*. New Haven: Yale University Press, 1950.

4. Otto, Rudolph, *The Idea of the Holy*. London: Oxford University Press, 1923.

5. Tillich, Paul, *Systematic Theology*. Chicago: University of Chicago Press, 1951. *Dynamics of Faith*. New York: Harper & Row, Publishers, 1957.

6. From a speech by Louis M. Orr, M. D. (President of A.M.A., 1959–1960), delivered before the Graduating class of Emory University, Atlanta, Georgia, June 6, 1960, *Vital Speeches* (Oct. 15, 1960).

VALUING AS RELIGIOUS EXPERIENCE

Editorial Comments

In Foster's article we again look closely at one of the areas of confrontation which constitutes in part the *raison d'être* for the whole study of values. The social institution of *religion* is very definitely under attack today, both internally and externally, both here and abroad. In this country, and in other countries as well, we see the authority of the Catholic Church being confronted internally by Catholics themselves over the issue of birth control. The values being appealed to in this issue coming from such different areas— theology, medicine, psychology, sociology—it is small wonder that a value conflict has resulted here. The Catholic Church also finds itself enmeshed in confrontations of an external nature as well. In Northern Ireland it is Protestants, not other Catholics, who are confronting Catholics, and in Viet Nam it is Buddhists who are doing the same. Protestants in this country, on the other hand, also find themselves involved in confrontations from within. The irony of "death of God" theologians holding forth from their teaching positions in Protestant seminaries supported by "the religious establishment" is hard to escape. Eternal confrontation in this country can be seen in the conflicts sometimes erupting between Black and Jew with epithets of "Anti-Semite" and "Jew Bigot" being exchanged. Moving from the ghetto to the courts, we also find an external confrontation, this time from challenges to the prayer-in-school rulings, tax-exempt status of churches, and the whole question of the separation of church and state.

On the international scene, in country after country Communist atheist confronts non-Communist theist, while in Africa and Asia Christian missionaries carrying what is often viewed as "the white man's burden" are being swept aside by waves of nationalism, hostile to anything felt to smack of Western paternalism, or worse yet, Western exploitation via neo-colonialism. Certainly religion, then, can be seen to be a hotbed of confrontation today, with the underlying value conflicts very close to the surface.

In Foster's article we find three main aspects of the value issue as it relates to religion. First, in echoing Bonner and Strunk, he raises the question as to why psychology has not itself valued the study of man's values, including his religious ones. Indeed, he indicts it on the grounds that it has "devoted so much of its energy in the past one hundred years to a taboo on valuing—*to the value of banishing value* from our conceptions of man and from our research methodology." In his reference to "our scientific methodology" he shows that a second value area must be considered, the area that questions which values should be used for judging the fruits of scientific research. Foster also touches on a third value area by bringing up some value theories (theories *about* values) themselves, especially Paul Tillich's. And here we see a good example of how such a theory might shed some light on some aspects of the many value conflicts underlying our confrontations today.

Using Tillich's concept of "ultimate concern," for instance, it might be observed that some of the Catholic laity objecting so vociferously over the birth control issue are perhaps ultimately concerned with the psychological well-being of their families. They value sex without fear of unwarranted pregnancy, spontaneous self-expression without guilt, personal choice without threat of condemnation. But such ultimate concern must necessarily fall on deaf ears when one is ultimately concerned with the revealed word of God as stated in the Holy Scripture as interpreted by his one true Church. Husbands quoting statistics on ulcers in married Catholic women to theologians quoting scriptural passages on the procreative function of the sacrament of marriage hardly seems the way to resolve the conflict. And as both sides become locked in on their positions and increase the hostility they feel for the other side, perhaps Tillich's concept of "idolatry" that Foster brings in could also give some insight into what is happening. When the laity walks out on one of its bishops during Mass in a protest demonstration over his stand on birth control, are they feeling an unconditioned Christian love for him? And does he feel such a love for them as he denounces their pride and arrogance and error from the pulpit? If the disagreement does not take place in such a context of love, understanding, and acceptance, what of the "ultimate concerns" that are responsible for this state of affairs?

Here, then, is just one example of how a theory that viewed valuing as essentially a process of religious experience at different levels might actually make a specific and concrete contribution to the analysis and possible solution of a real-life confrontation stemming from a conflict in values.

In Knight's article which follows we will see how a particular value theory actually is used in such a way, for while Foster was talking about religious experience and the valuing process in a broad and general way, Knight speaks of a very specific religious confrontation and introduces a particular value theory in an effort to help resolve the conflict inherent in this confrontation. The conflict in question is "the new morality."

10

ON THE MATURING PROCESS

The Relationship of Values to Adolescent Development*

JAMES A. KNIGHT

Recently an adolescent patient mentioned how confused he was regarding a proper set of moral principles to adopt and to follow. He mentioned the new morality and situation ethics which he and his friends were interpreting as "make your own rules." He described the multiple and often contradictory voices in the field of moral teachings as a present-day Tower of Babel with its confusion of tongues. He expressed a need for some well-worked-out system of values which he could examine and then accent or modify in the light of his conscience. He implied that he saw everywhere uncertainty and instability about values.

This adolescent is probably typical of today's youth. Some important ingredients are lacking for their proper development, and they are searching for substitutes to compensate for the deficiencies. For example, such deficiencies account in part for the attraction of psychedelic drugs. Recently, a 17 year old, in writing the editor of *Time* (11, p. 10) stated that society had rebelled against and

* Most of this material has appeared previously in the author's book *Conscience and Guilt*. New York: Appleton-Century-Crofts, 1969. Permission has been granted by the publisher to use the material.

turned its back on love, individuality, and humanity. To get a better perspective of things he was looking forward to experiencing the psychedelic field. He emphasized that he wanted to get "inside things, in the mainstream, bloodstream—sightsee the system so to speak." He wanted to explore countries that most people have only sailed around.* One can only conclude that it is a sad commentary on the institutions and agencies of society which have failed to let this young man know that the most exalting experiences in life can be genuine and that drug-induced experiences only simulate the real ones. Falling in love, a conversion or religious experience, self-mastery, the wonders of the natural world, and a host of other phenomena furnish dimensions to living richer by far than psychedelic drugs.

Teaching Morality

The question is often asked, "Can we teach morality?" Although the capacity for conscience is innate, and although there are dimensions of conscience that extend beyond mere socialization, much of the content and application of conscience come from the family and society.† Thus the child needs to be introduced to the higher value system of the group in which he is living. Where instruction is not given or where the family and society have become uncertain of basic values and consequently have developed a collective instability and uncertainty about values, one sees a developmental defect in the spiritual and moral dimension of man. Bruno Bettelheim reminds us: ". . . contrary to some people's opinion, youth does not create its own cause for which it is ready to fight. All it can do is to embrace causes developed by mature men" (2).

---

* In sharp contrast to this young man's philosophy is that of the distinguished young composer David Amram, who speaks of the body as the vessel of the soul. If it is in shape, it tunes the mind. He stated that when he was writing his opera, *Twelfth Night*, he ran 60 laps around the Y.M.C.A. gym track every day. "It cleared my mind. By not smoking, drinking, or using drugs I find I can be high all the time on life" (9, pp. 33–36).

† Robert Ardrey in his book, *African Genesis*, stresses his view that civilization has come to mankind through the observance of nature's most ancient law, that commanding order. And that this instinct for order is humanity's most reliable ally and is much broader and more universal than conscience. Ardrey points out the provinciality of conscience in that its code and content come from one's particular clan or group and therefore may lack universality (1).

The statement is often made about the difficult time every developing person must have in our society to acquire a proper sense of morality and a value system worthy of total commitment. Three major agencies contribute to the moral development: his family, his age group or peers, and the larger community with its three principal institutions of school, church, and mass media (books, newspapers, magazines, movies, radio, television). The development of responsible behavior represents a careful blending of personal responsibility and outer controls which are furnished by agencies such as the family and school. As the child grows, there is an expected decrease in outer controls and an increase in his own responsibility as a person. Thus, in healthy growth the individual experiences a conscience transformation in that his inner controls are strengthened and consolidated and take on a guiding, monitoring, and sustaining role in conduct and human relationships.

Thus, morality provides a core integrative mechanism for the development of personality. Morality is much more than a question of prohibitions but rather is concerned with the values and definitions of appropriate behavior by which the individual governs his actions. Morality then as a part of the structure of the self concerns itself with defining and directing one's life in accord with the values one has chosen. Erikson has summarized well the leavening quality of morality in society as one's ethical acts touch another: "The true ethical sense of the young adult at its best encompasses moral restraint and ideal vision, while insisting on concrete commitments to those intimate relationships and work associations by which man can hope to share a lifetime of productivity and competence. Truly ethical acts enhance a mutuality between the doer and the other— a mutuality which strengthens the doer even as it strengthens the other. Thus, the "doer unto" and "the other" are one deed. Developmentally this means that the doer is activated in whatever strength is appropriate to his age, stage, and condition, even as he activates in the other the strength appropriate to his age, stage, and condition" (3).

Values and Development

Among the many tasks which a youngster usually accomplishes as he moves toward adulthood, two relate particularly to values:

the consolidation of his pattern of internal controls and the construction of an individual moral philosophy. He is faced with learning to live with heightened impulses, as well as finding a balance between desire and restraint. Then he must build a system of values which will serve as a guide to conduct and valuation appropriate to his circumstances, and which will not be just an imitation of what he has been told to believe. Although he can fail in one or the other of these tasks, healthy development depends on successful accomplishment in both, for controls and values are closely linked.

There are several areas in which youth carry out explorations, using every medium at their disposal, in their search for the type of person they want to be. Among the significant areas are religion, sex, and social idealism.

Rebellion and Re-building: Religion can have an important part to play in the acquisition of an appropriate value system by the developing person. The religious area appeals to youth as a medium for orienting themselves, and often reflects their attempt to establish themselves as individuals with their own identity and personal set of values.

The adolescent, as a part of his movement toward independence, feels constrained to examine and reconstruct the religious beliefs given him by his family. He may discard certain of the religious beliefs of childhood as he struggles in his search for his own set of values and his own identity. In order to become fully emancipated from his parents, it is usually necessary for the adolescent to doubt the religious attitudes, standards, and value system of his parents. Involvement with and support from his peers involve the adolescent in a comparison of his religious beliefs with those of others. Such a comparison usually results in some change, ranging from abandonment to renewed intensity.

A further word is indicated in reference to the adolescent's rebellion against the religion he has been taught. In actuality the rebellion is often against what he thought was taught him. He is rejecting chiefly his own childhood conceptions, for which he may illogically blame his culture, parents, and church. Many years may pass before he realizes that his rebellion was not so much against parents, church, or culture as against his own immaturity. Not many things can be as upsetting to parents as an adolescent, struggling with emancipation, attacking the treasured value system of his parents.

Adolescents have a need to be exposed to some structure or order of religious beliefs that they can interiorize for themselves or reject. In many adolescents there is such confusion and ignorance about religion that they are unable to deal with the specific traditions in their background. In other words, permissiveness and obscurity in religion give the adolescent nothing to rebel against or to be dependent upon.

The predicament today seems to have been summarized well by Kenneth P. Landon, director of the Center for South and Southeast Asian Studies at American University: "I grew up in an era when it was still respectable to say 'Lord, I believe. Help thou my unbelief.' Now it is more in style to say, 'Lord, I don't believe much. Help thou my use of cybernetics in determining my probabilities and options' " (8, p. 1). In such a society the adolescent's religious conflicts may not find resolution as readily as in a society with a more structured value orientation.

The institutional church appears to be needed only in a limited way by the adolescent. The group life is important when it offers opportunities and activities involving his peers. The basic ideals and standards of behavior promulgated by the church offer the adolescent a sense of structure or permanence amid the changes and inconsistencies of everyday life.

The adolescent needs some sharp directions, while being permitted the freedom to make mistakes. The church has often succeeded in encouraging the adolescent not to fear the independence of moral judgment that must attend age and experience. Fortunately, some churches are abandoning rigid codes of do's and don't's in the area of soical behavior such as dating, and are promoting educational programs of self-knowledge and the dynamics of personal, responsible love.

The adolescent seeks in the pastor of the church a person who helps him with the tension growing out of unattained ideals or unreached moral goals. The good pastor is acutely aware that each person must stumble to find his way in love, although he has a clear ideal before him. If the adolescent's conscience, however, points in a direction different from the pastor's, the pastor can search with him in dialogue but not preach to him in absolutes. The adolescent is open to direction but not to dictation.

The pastor is often rendered ineffectual as a counseling resource for adolescents if they see the pastor's job as one of condemnation rather than acceptance and consolation. Often the church deals with social and behavioral problems through eradication. For example, if confronted with problem drinking the church's solution has frequently been to vote the county dry. If confronted with sexual promiscuity, then laws are passed regarding prostitution, curfews, and so on. Instead of accepting and dealing creatively with persons who participate in questionable activities, the church frequently rejects with condemnation. Such an approach has devastating implications for counseling, for if the church's major way of solving problems is through condemnation, a young person may consider the pastor as the last possible source of help when social mistakes are made.

Recently, a psychiatrist mentioned that at breakfast on a Sunday morning his adolescent son announced his atheism. Prior to that he had considered the ministry as a vocation. About the same time another physician's son, who had also considered the ministry as a vocation, announced his atheism. It was discovered later that these two newly avowed atheists were friends and had been in discussion with one another on religious matters. Both sets of parents were deeply troubled and wondered what was happening in the thinking of their sons.

It is not uncommon for an adolescent to enter a stage of atheism or probably what is better defined as agnosticism. The meaning of this fairly common experience in adolescence probably has something to do with the individual's previous relationship to both his father and God.

In the small child, the being called God is probably conceived as being human and not spiritual, for the supreme value is found in the parents. Freud attempted to show in *The Future of an Illusion* (6) that the idea of God was no more than an infantile picture of the father. Many take issue with Freud for seeming to forget that the father might also be for the child the carrier of the projection of the God image, as Carl Jung would express it. Thus, it is probably natural that the child's religious experience should be bound up with the parents. If development proceeds normally, his projections onto them are gradually withdrawn with the result that they become to him more human and less divine.

Many a young person during adolescence is not yet mature enough in his religion to distinguish between God and father. During adolescence, one of his tasks is to separate God from father. To accomplish this, he involves himself in struggles with authority for freedom and independence. In order to clarify his confusion and begin his movement toward independence, he may reject God or father, or possibly both. After that, he may begin working through his rebellion and arrive at a new understanding of and relationship to God and father. Religion then is used in an appropriate and not conflictive manner.

Sexuality. Although focused on strongly by the adult world, genital sex is only a part of multi-faceted sexuality of youth. In the developing person sexuality serves broader purposes than genitality. This is especially true in his quest for identity and in his expression of social consciousness. These two facets of sexuality are emphasized in this discussion because of their profound relevance to the emerging value system in youth.

In Erikson's analysis of the developmental tasks of adolescence and early adulthood, the problem of individual identity is put before that of intimacy (4, pp. 56–121). Unless the outlines of an adolescent's individual being have been established and fortified, intimacy may bring psychological fragmentation. Thus, the general rule evolves, that in healthy development, identity must precede intimacy. Often the young person reverses the process and tries to affirm his identity through intimacy. The reversal has less dire consequences for the girl than for the boy. Probably this is true because the girl often achieves in some degree intimacy before she develops the kind of continuity and integrity of self which an identity resolution implies. Thus, it is not uncommon for a psychotherapist to see a girl who has gained a developed identity in consequence of intimacy rather than as a precursor of it. Through intimate connections with others, the girl may come to know her own individuality and to solve the question of who she is. This reversal in girls relates partly to social reality. Our culture emphasizes so strongly for the girl the need to marry that she hardly has time or energy to invest in identity-resolution until she has gained a measure of security in a stable love relationship.

Thus, the girl usually arrives at identity resolutions through the interpersonal and after she has attained a relatively satisfactory integration of intimacy and the erotic. The boy's situation is quite different in that his identity depends on his achieving autonomy and an acceptable integration of assertiveness and self-direction.

The difference between boys and girls, in identity formation, has been somewhat overstated for emphasis. To put the difference simply, a basic feminine goal is to form a lasting tie to another, and is not an individual achievement in the sense that the boy's vocational goal is. Yet for both sexes, the capacity for a mature sexual relationship is intimately linked with a sense of personal identity.

Possibly our society is cheating youth of one of their most precious heritages by letting the sexual flower, figuratively speaking, be picked when it is only a bud, thus never reaching the splendor of its full bloom. Society's intense preoccupation with genital sexuality has created both moral and identity problems for the developing person in that free sexual expression appears to be encouraged on all sides. Our sex-oriented culture may be the result of many factors, among them our worship of youth and all that is young and virile, and a denial of, or depreciation of old age and even of the wisdom born of years.

Part of our society in its efforts to control sexuality seems inadvertently to call undue attention to it. As many have pointed out, when a group insists on suppressing the sex instinct in everything the group betrays the fact that it really sees that instinct in everything. Along with the inhibitors, with their unintentional advertising, there are the exploiters of sex—those who use it to sell merchandise of every kind. Recently I saw a truck from an oyster dealer in New Orleans that had printed on its side in large letters, "Eat oysters and love longer." Thus, youth are led to believe that potency and sex appeal are at the center of our value system.

A dimension of sexuality in youth, often puzzling to adults, is the social consciousness which is linked to *eros* (10, pp. 436–46). Nothing is more evident in the adolescent than a heightened sense of the erotic. Simultaneously one usually sees a widening and deepening of the ocean of goodwill. The different types of love sustain, feed, and strengthen one another in the adolescent, for he does not separate *eros* from *agapé*. The feeling of love that permeates his life, that helps him relate to the opposite sex, is closely akin to the feeling that is his love for God or a Higher Being. When he carries a sign saying, "make love, not war," his activity may appear depraved to many adults. But is it? The adolescent's involvement in social reforms, sit-ins, and picket lines is not a renunciation of genital sexuality or a sublimation of the libido but an expression of the same driving force in his life.

In an adolescent's love for his girl, God becomes close, maybe for the first time, through the prism of the relationship. The beloved one is often the only person who can make God seem real. Maybe the adolescent is re-emphasizing for us an ancient truth that one must know love if he is to know God.

The adult, in contrast to the adolescent, usually distinguishes sharply between *eros* and *agapé* and draws a clear line between genital sexuality and social consciousness. Probably it is adult psychopathology that has created a great deal of sexual conflict in the growing person. It is refreshing to see youth wed *eros* with *agapé*.

The potential for idealism in regard to sexual life, and the dignity that it should have, has been limited to the sexual without bringing in the much wider dimension of personal love, the totality with which love engages the whole of one's personality. Because there has been such a fragmentation or a differentiation made in the various approaches to love, the one has suffered at the expense of the other. The problem of integrating the sexual with human and divine love is the urgent problem of our day.

Social Idealism. In the inner struggles which erupt at puberty, social concerns appear to be an important part of the young person's life. The reasons for human existence are heatedly debated. The desire to do something to improve the world is conspicuously present and often expresses itself in a concern for world peace. The religious man who fights for social justice may become his ideal. As one would suspect, the psychological origins of the adolescent's religio-social idealism lie in part in his yearning for peace within himself. Through the mental mechanism of projecting his inner turmoil onto the outer world, his yearning for peace within himself may take the form of a wish for world peace and social accord. Upheaval in the outer world intensifies the inner conflict of the adolescent, for he needs the steadying influence of moral strength and unity in the world around him. A stable environment helps immensely in meeting the emotional needs of the conflict-ridden youngster. Also, religious observances with festive ceremonies and meaningful symbols introduce a stable rhythm into the adolescent's family and community life.

Recently in a study I carried out with a hundred college students (7, pp. 31–50), a number of them spoke of conflicts related to social issues. Hypocrisy of religious parents and other socially responsible people in regard to social issues caused pain and confusion. What was most disturbing was the effort of the "faithful" to bend the biblical teachings to fit their hates, prejudices, or bigotry. The adolescents stated that they would have been less shaken in their struggles if the adult world had acknowledged religious precepts as ideal, and at the same time acknowledged their inability to attain the ideal in their actions. But twisting or distorting the structure of religious morality and idealism, the adolescents felt, left them with no fixed point on which to orient their values or conduct. At the same time, they, themselves, often found that it was easy for them to profess one thing and act in another way. In such circumstances, when their consciences ached, they found a little comfort in meditating on the hypocrisies of religious people, including their parents.

In the young person's search for inner harmony nothing is more helpful than an adult example of mutual understanding, cooperative living, and devotion to the principles of equality of all human beings. Respect for personality, regard for the rights and feelings of others, and commitment to the common good represent moral and spiritual values. Effective spiritual-moral commitment is the only safe and hopeful way of giving youth the structure of social peace needed for them to find inner peace.

Conclusion

The impression today is that pleasure comes only from the erotic, immoral, and unlawful, and the pursuit of it is "smart" and "in." Not much support is given to the thesis that pleasure can come from self-mastery and self-discipline. Yet stories such as that presented in the *Bridge Over the River Kwai* strike a responsive chord in youth, because they see a higher value in the disciplined life than they have ever known.

Unfortunately, new developments in both religion and psychiatry have been branded as promoting permissiveness in morality. Many young people interpret the new morality as affirming no established standards but declaring that *all* decisions are relative. The death of God theology, usually through a misinterpretation of its meaning, may be removing a source of both judgment and strength. Because of its nonjudgmental attitude, psychiatry is often accused of moral indifference.

Where then will youth turn for certitude amid doubt, for light hidden in shadows? Whether they declare themselves indifferent agnostics or militant atheists they will continue to have psychological needs for direction, for a message of redemptive hope, and a kind of sanction that some things are eternal. And regardless of the freedom they may demand, most of them feel more comfortable if limits are set, if some guidelines are evident, and if the adult world cares enough about them to help them avoid disaster.

Some day they may discover that the new morality seeks only to free them from a torturous and impossible obedience to rigid, external standards in order that true morality can emerge through their own nature as they are made increasingly aware of their own depths and of the extension of these depths beyond themselves. In situation ethics or the new morality, law is reduced from a statutory system of rules to the love canon alone. Precepts are replaced with the living principles of *agapé* in the sense of goodwill at work in partnership with reason (5).

Also, hopefully youth will learn that psychiatry is not morally indifferent nor does it advocate uninhibited self-indulgence. It is rethinking its position on the causes of crime, delinquency, and other forms of antisocial behavior and is questioning the assumption of relating antisocial behavior to emotional illness or extremes of poverty, rather than to the absence of, or to faulty, value education. Psychiatry is fully aware that if religious, social, and moral values are not presented to children in their formative years, then they most likely will lack them. Also, psychiatry is aware that in its efforts to understand and explain antisocial actions it has not worked equally as hard in urging that such actions be controlled and restricted.

In the young person's search for acceptable values and controls, probably at no stage in his life should he be free from creative tension regarding morality. The individual must continually balance and weigh his actions in terms of how generally recognized absolute values can be put into action in the context of his group's values and his own personal values.

Morality can never be completely an individual matter because of its interdependence with group morality. Thus, the individual's moral commitments are influenced by his social matrix and the judgments and evaluations of his peers. His behavior is integrated by the moral commitments to himself and to his society according to a whole range of social values.

In his search for his value system, the adolescent mentioned earlier finds around him only a Tower of Babel with its confusion of tongues. In spite of this serious indictment of our society, many of this adolescent's peers are able to tune out discordant voices and are identifying the constructive forces they need to acquire and consolidate a mature morality. Such an accomplishment in our present type of world says something special about the essential nature of man.

REFERENCES

1. Ardrey, Thomas, *African Genesis—A Personal Investigation into the Animal Origins and Nature of Man*. New York: Atheneum Publishers, 1966.

2. Bettelheim, Bruno, "The Problem of Generations," *Daedalus* (Winter, 1962).

3. Erikson, Erik, "The Golden Rule and the Cycle of Life," *Harvard Medical Alumni Bulletin* (Winter, 1963).

4. Erikson, Erik, "The Problem of Ego Identity," *Journal of the American Psychoanalytic Association*, Vol. 4 (1956).

5. Fletcher, Joseph, *Situation Ethics: The New Morality*. Philadelphia; the Westminster Press, 1966.

6. Freud, Sigmund, *The Future of an Illusion*, trans. J. Strachey, Standard Edition, Vol. 21. London: Hogarth Press, 1961.

7. Knight, James A., "Religious-Psychological Conflicts of the Adolescent," in *Adolescence, Care and Counseling*, ed. Gene L. Usdin. Philadephia: J. B. Lippincott Co., 1967.

8. Landon, K. P., "The Eternal Verities," *Family Forum* (Oct. 1966).

9. "Close-up/David Amram, a Rising American Composer," *Life* (August 11, 1967).

10. Seeley, John R., *The Americanization of the Unconscious*. New York: International Science Press, 1967.

11. *Time* (July 21, 1967), "Letters" section.

THE RELATIONSHIP OF VALUES TO ADOLESCENT DEVELOPMENT

Editorial Comments

Knight helps us to examine the moral and spiritual development of our youth as it is silhouetted against "the new morality." In an overview we can see on the one side of the conflict the religious establishment, symbolizing a commitment to *legalism*, to the existence of universal and absolute moral values. Of the other possible positions on the other side of the conflict, three are of relevance here. First, there is the *antinomian* position, which simply denies legalism by asserting that there are no universal absolute values, none at all. Second, there is the *new morality* position, which affirms that there are absolute values, but denies that they are universal. Thus, there *is* an absolute moral demand made upon the individual by agapic love, but it is *unique*, not universal, since the situation in which the individual finds himself is necessarily unique (and thus the synonymous term for the new morality, "situation ethics"). And third, there is Knight's own position in which he attempts to avoid both the universalism of legalism and the nihilism of antinomianism by modifying the position of the new morality because of some realistic considerations he feels it has overlooked. An examination of the reasoning behind these modifications is quite enlightening, for it will clearly show the interplay between a theory *about* value and a theory *of* value.

Knight observes that "psychiatry is aware that in its efforts to understand and explain antisocial actions [*a theory about value*], it has not worked equally hard in urging that such actions be controlled and restricted [*a theory of value*]." In attempting to build an adequate theory *of* value, Knight first goes to a theory *about* value, more specifically, a theory about the valuing process in the development of the adolescent. On the basis of this theory, which he obviously feels can be supported by scientific research, he maintains that what the new morality proposes on a *normative* basis is impossible on a *factual* basis. He feels that it demands an individuality in matters of morals which is impossible because individual morality is interdependent with group morality. "Thus, the individual's moral commitments are influenced by his social matrix and the judgments and evaluations of his peers. His behavior is integrated by the moral commitments to himself and to his society according to a whole range of social values." Whether one agrees with him or not, of course, the really important thing right here lies in understanding how a theory *about* value can influence the formulation of a theory *of* value.

When one looks, then, at some of the confrontations based on conflicts over religious values which are currently creating so much tension in our midst, the need for research such as Knight's becomes obvious indeed. Consider two of the many problem areas confronting adolescents today, in which religious values play an important part: sex and war. Fornication is absolutely wrong, a sin against the law of God; fornication is alright if you want to do it, an individual thing solely between the parties involved; fornication is sometimes right and sometimes wrong, depending on the depth of the love commitments on both sides and the appropriateness of intercourse as a creative medium for expressing this love. Killing in war is always wrong, a transgression against one of God's commandments as well as Christ's injunction to love everyone; killing in war is perfectly justified if you believe in it, a patriotic act with respect to one's duty to his country, a loving act with respect to those one wishes to protect; killing in war is sometimes right and sometimes wrong, depending upon the individuals actually involved in the situation and one's commitments to them, and upon the other unique variables that characterize this particular situation. Old morality? New morality? No morality? The confrontations are upon us. The value conflicts are obvious. Any help, such as Knight's, in attempting to resolve the dilemma is greatly needed.

In the editor's article which follows, we return to another one of those original areas of confrontation which started off our investigation into the value issue: the area of education.

II

ON THE ROLE OF EDUCATION

Classroom Behavior as a Function of Value Motivation

JEREMIAH W. CANNING

Those who are avid football fans as I am are no doubt familiar with the malady attributed to some quarterbacks of "hearing footsteps." These unfortunate individuals evidently have been smeared so badly by 250-pound blitzing linebackers on occasion that whenever they drop back to pass they are unable to keep their minds fully on the task at hand, nervously imagining that disaster is about to overtake them from some unseen quarter at any moment. I must admit that I am reminded of this type of situation whenever I get together with fellow faculty members or with college administrators these days. The academic version of the "hearing footsteps" syndrome consists of nervously wondering when the next student demonstration or rash of "student power" demands will hit your campus.

What makes this so much worse is the very frustrating feeling that the whole thing is out of your hands, that an irrational fate just might happen to inflict upon your campus a Berkeley, or Co-

lumbia, or San Francisco State type episode for no apparent reason
whatsoever. Lamentable this state of affairs may well be, but sur-
prising it certainly is not. When we actually take a look at what's
been passing for a college education all these years, the surprise is
not that student dissent has started to occur, but that it has just
started to occur. Surely most of the things students are now rebelling against have been there all along. It is the thesis of this paper
that there is much that needs rebelling against and I hope to be able
to spell out what I feel is undesirable about certain aspects of our
present educational set-up, as well as at least point in the direction
of a possible solution. I do not wish, however, to discuss in any way
whether or not some forms of student action are appropriate means
of expressing protest against these things that I will be considering.
While I feel that usually (though not always) students put their
fingers on real wrongs that need to be righted, I also feel that
usually (though not always) they go about it in a somewhat immature and unwise manner (though it hardly seems shocking that
youths not fully mature or completely wise should act this way).
But I am afraid that if we should discuss the matter of "how should
students protest," we would miss the point altogether of "what
needs protesting against." Therefore, it is wholly with the latter
issue that this paper will be concerned.

The analysis that is to follow will be four-fold, as I will be
looking at two different things from two different viewpoints. The
two things I have in mind are classroom behavior and the motivation
that is to a large extent responsible for it; the two viewpoints are the
descriptive and the normative ones. Thus, I will be discussing both
typical classroom behavior and the motivation behind it as we
actually do find them, and also classroom behavior and motivation
as we *ideally should* find them. I will present my ideal set of motives
first, then contrast with it the motives and behavior we actually
find in the classroom setting, and finally draw out the practical
behavioral consequences that follow from the type of motivation
I am recommending as ideal.

There are six main aspects of ideal classroom motivation which
I will mention (although I quickly add that these are not "the
magic six" since they are too broad, overlapping each other somewhat, as well as too narrow, leaving out some things that are very
definitely relevant).

The first of these six is *a desire to search for the truth*. I am fully aware of the very romantic connotations connected with such a notion. Indeed, I have had to resist the strong temptation to hedge my point by translating my search for "the truth" into something more palatable to professional philosophers—such as my search for "synthetic statements ultimately reducible without remainder via correspondence rules to finite conjunctions of observation statements that have been directly confirmed by empirical evidence" (may logical positivism continue to rest in peace!). But this isn't really what I want to say at all. So I will keep my old bromide "search for the truth," for while I am more than willing to give up the simple-minded aspects usually associated with such a quest, I very definitely am not willing to give up the idea of the passionate commitment to the attainment of knowledge that such a phrase brings to mind. Thus, the scientist who strives to see the facts as they really are regardless of any pressure brought to bear upon him, the existentialist who tries to transvalue his culture in order to attain self-awareness, and the Hippie who desires simply to "tell it as it is," all would fall under my heading of individuals who are "searching for the truth." Now I hope it is obvious by the above examples that I am not begging any questions by speaking of "the truth." What the truth is might be anything. It could be the truth of the skeptic that the only thing we can know is that we cannot know anything else, or the truth of the relativist that all truths, except for this one, are only relative to a particular time and place, or the truths of any one of a countless number of other possible positions. All I am suggesting is that it is desirable in a classroom setting for students and professor alike to wish to find out the way things are, whatever way that may turn out to be.

My second ideal motivation is that of *desiring to be oneself*. This would mean that all concerned should feel comfortable in the classroom situation, saying what they think and expressing what they feel. The class should consist of a group of unique individuals who are not afraid to be individuals, and who are accepted by all the others as individuals.

Third, there should be *a strong attempt to be as intellectually rigorous as possible*. Positions should be presented as clearly, as concisely, as consistently, and as comprehensively as can be. And again, there is no begging the question involved, for while reality itself might well be unclear, extremely complex, contradictory, or incomprehensible, one's theories about it need not be. One certainly can state clearly just how unclear things are.

A fourth ideal motive consists of *the desire to deal with the material studied on an emotional level as well as an intellectual one.* Thus, the course content would be psychologically real to the individuals concerned, with theories given practical applications and abstractions tied down to real life situations. All this would make the matters studied "living hypotheses," rather than "dead" ones, to use James' phrase.

Fifth, ideally one should also wish *to establish some sense of community with the educational group of which he is a member.* In this way a class wouldn't consist of just a collection of individuals; rather, a group rapport involving both a mutual sharing and a mutual caring could occur.

Sixth and last, *one should be motivated by a desire for the class setting itself, when appropriate, to be a real life encounter in its own right,* rather than just an artificial structure where one always learns *about* X, but never *does* X. In this way things worth talking about would not always be brought in from "outside" to be taken apart, put back together again, and then related to "the real world." Class itself would be part, sometimes the most important part, of the real world. The academic environment could then function as the setting for an existential "happening" and students and faculty would not be forced to look for such stimulation and challenge elsewhere.

So what would a class of ideally motivated students and faculty members be like? It would consist of a real community of unique individuals who freely express themselves in their commitment to the truth, and who deal with matters of concern right on the spot as they come up in an intellectually rigorous and emotionally open way.

Let us now shift from the normative realm to the descriptive, and I will attempt to state what I feel the *actual* motives found in the classroom are, and also what type of *actual* behavior I think stems from these motives. Suppose we enter a typical college classroom and encounter some students and a professor. What might they be there for? To "search for the truth?" Perhaps, but more often than not, unfortunately, we find the students, at least, searching for the almighty grade. Or a bit better, but not much, searching for "the facts." After all, the professor has spent all those extra years in graduate school learning what the facts are, so his obvious function in the class is to communicate these facts to his students. On occasion the facts might actually be interesting, or entertaining, and sometimes they might even prove useful later on from a strictly vocational standpoint, but most of the time they must be learned "simply because they're there." Students and professors together pretty much assume that education is concerned with "covering the ground" in a particular discipline. Thus, when we enter a classroom we should not be surprised to find an entire roomful of stenographers, not students, busily scribbling down whatever the professor has to say. If the professor is a bad one he dully reads his old graduate school notes to his students. If he is a good one and has thereby developed his own lecture material in which he is very interested, he still more or less presents it to the class to digest until time to regurgitate it on an exam. The best digestors with the most regurgitation get the best grades, of course, for after all, that's what education's all about. So who can search for truth when "the ground" must be covered?

Suppose that we look for a moment at the actual individuals who are taking up space in this classroom. What hits us immediately is that while there are, obviously, different bodies in the room it is not at all obvious just what characteristics differentiate the possessors of these bodies as people. They all appear to be hiding behind the myriad of social roles that society has been handing them throughout their lives. For example, the students must remember that they constitute "the younger generation," the professor "the older," and for that reason alone, they must give him the proper respect. The professor, since he is the authority figure in the class, must make sure that the students "remember their place" and don't get so close to him so that his authority is threatened. The students in turn attempt to "psych out" the professor so they "know what he wants to hear" and can thus manipulate him successfully in order to obtain the grades they desire. The professor, of course, since he is usually also married and has children, must carefully lead his group of slightly irresponsible child-surrogates with all the fatherly wisdom he can muster. And so it goes, with each one attempting to "play the game"—if he were only sure just what it was. But who

are these people *really?* Who knows? They want to stay hidden
in order not to expose themselves as they really are, so should it be
any wonder that in the classroom situation one can't spot the real
individuals behind the collection of masks they wear?

Let us press further, now, and attempt to examine the intellectual commitment evident in this classroom. For the most part,
we find students who don't push their profs, and profs who don't
push their students. Thinking is too much trouble and is sometimes
even dangerous, and it is so much easier to simply listen, understand,
memorize, recite, and then forget. Since neither students nor professor have to think to get by, why should they? Developing one's
own thinking on a particular issue doesn't necessarily merit recognition, the way the system is set up, so what's the point in it?

Emotional involvement within this classroom setting seems even
harder to find than intellectual. Express how you *feel* about something that matters to you in front of people who might laugh at
you, or possibly attack you for your feelings, or at best simply be
embarrassed for you for baring your soul in public? It's a well
known fact that if one takes things too seriously one gets all psychologically upset, so it's much better to keep an appropriate dis-
tance between the individual and the material he is studying. It's
so much safer to disarm potentially dangerous emotional questions
with a nice, purely intellectual, objective, dispassionate, "Well, it
is interesting, of course, and all that, but after all . . ." So while
the level of intellectual involvement in the class is usually low
enough, the level of emotional involvement is even lower.

Examining the group further, for a possible sense of community,
we have a hard time finding one. Of course Greeks from the same
house do tend to stick together pretty much, as do sweethearts,
majors in the discipline the course is in, and a few others, but that's
about it. There's just about as much feeling as in a movie house
where there are many people who don't know each other, all watching the same movie. Only the aggressive and relatively articulate
students ever say much in class and they constitute a very small
fraction of the group's entire population. And usually the dialogue
goes on in the form of student-question/professor-answer, with
little or no interaction among the students themselves. But then
most people aren't in the class to interact with others, for after all,
others place demands on one. And while it's true that one can't get

any support from a roomful of separate egos, neither, at least, is there any danger from them.

From what has gone before, it is quite obvious that there is little chance of this classroom setting being a real learning situation for those involved. Most don't really want it to be and it isn't. So instead of the group talking about its problems that are relevant to the course and attempting to solve them, the discussion leans towards other groups from other cultures or from other periods in our own culture. All the action that is worthwhile is going on someplace else, and at best is only referred to indirectly in class.

Now that I have completed my academician's chamber of horrors, let us move on to consider the alternatives previously recommended. I have only given the motivational side of my picture thus far, and if I were to stop with this, I might carry the day by default. However, this would really not be fair, for the true test of a theory is not how pretty it seems as it floats abstractly on high, but how well it fares when it is tied down to the human level and tested by the value of its practical consequences. Therefore, let me give six examples from my own experience which point up *problems* which can arise when the motives which I consider to be ideal prevail. I could give many examples where everything worked beautifully, of course, but anyone can support his position in such a manner and much more than this is needed. It is the really tough cases that need skillful handling, not only for their own sakes, but also for the sake of potential future successes which might never be realized if these other cases are allowed to ruin the opportunities for such realization.

First, let's take the noble ideal of searching for the truth and see what can happen sometimes on the behavioral level when it is taken seriously. In one seminar in contemporary philosophy I taught, there was one student who felt this whole idea of searching for the truth was nothing but naiveté to the nth power. He said so openly while becoming involved in extremely heated controversies with the other members of the class who took the opposing position. Finally, things came to a head and the other members of the class voted that this one "nonsearcher" be removed from the class, whether he liked it or not, on the grounds that the group could not really progress toward its avowed goal with this foot-dragger along. They felt that evicting him would only symbolically represent what was already an established fact, namely, that he was *not* a member of the group, despite appearances, since he did not share the common commitment to really search for the truth. A unique and challenging solution, to say the least, but consider explaining to a university dean the principle behind removing a "student in good standing" from a class for which he had all the catalogue prerequisites, which he also happened to need to fulfill his major requirements, and which he had attended regularly while completing all the assignments, exams, and term papers. Unfortunately, we cannot take the Hollywood way out and have the student undergo a fantastic catharsis with the other students, after which he changes his personality completely and turns into the greatest truth searcher of them all, everyone living happily ever after. Instead, we must accept the following as "givens" in the situation and then come up with a workable solution: the student doesn't change, he continues to rebel, loudly and frequently, against the motivation of the group, the prof can't reach him, the other students continue to resent him strongly and to be inhibited by him, and the dean feels that everyone is being intolerant of him simply because he doesn't share their views, thus violating the principle of academic freedom.

Now, to cite a situation that developed from the tactic of allowing students to be themselves. One year we had a professor of philosophy and religion from another institution lecture to our student body on "the new morality" in contemporary Christian theology. Afterward, I asked him to meet with an honors seminar I was teaching in which we had discussed this particular position. One girl in the class happened to be the focal point of considerable campus gossip concerning homosexuality, but no one knew for sure whether or not the rumors had any basis in fact. Many felt the issue to be decided, however, when the girl, involved in a complex debate with the visiting professor over meaningful ways of expressing unconditioned Christian love for another human being, stated that she didn't see why going to bed with some of her girl friends couldn't be a perfectly meaningful way to express this type of love. The girl left the University at the end of the semester, but at least she had had the satisfaction of having felt comfortable enough in one class to express herself openly. Again, no Hollywood answers, please. He who encourages at least partial holidays for psychic censors should expect things to be brought up as a matter of course which are definitely not of the socially acceptable variety.

With regard to my recommendation for rigorous intellectual demands on students, there was the time I reported to a class Baruch Spinoza's position on the mind-body dualism which, I said, every fool knows is contained in his great major work, the *Ethic*. This was on Friday; on Monday one of my intellectual hard-chargers reported to the class that she had read the entire work twice over the weekend and that the views I attributed to Spinoza were neither stated nor implied there. She thereby concluded that I was either intellectually dishonest or intellectually irresponsible. You can be sure that I read over the work even more carefully than she but, unfortunately, with the same results. He who chooses to live by the sword of scholarly accuracy may also have to die by it sometime.

In attempting to make course content relevant to students' lives, the following situation occurred. Last year in an introductory class in ethics we started off with Sartre's idea of existential commitment, and had moved on to Eric Fromm's views on how to rid oneself of an authoritarian conscience, when one of my students simply dropped out of school and disappeared with not so much as a word to anyone, including his parents. Later I found out that all of the material we had talked about in class had become very real to him and that he had felt that he had to commit himself to a way of life completely different from his parents' way, but in a setting that would allow him to lessen the effects of their authoritarian conscience on him. He ended up in Haight-Ashbury for a while, and then Mexico. At present no one knows where he is. The only book he took with him, I found out, was one of his ethics texts, which I suppose makes everything all right.

For my fifth example—which pertains to the "sense of community with the educational group"—there is the case of the seminar on Paul Tillich which I taught with a colleague in Religion. The group had uncommon unity and before long the seminar seemed to be going on continuously even outside of regular class meetings. But as some of the individuals began to take things more and more seriously, they began to send out more and more calls for help to some of the others. Answering such calls not only took quite a toll timewise, but also tended to drain some of the individuals considerably from an emotional standpoint. Trying to bail people out who had just come face to face with the "threat of nonbeing" was not exactly fun and games for anyone but, of course, when one is really committed to others, what else does he do? A real community feeling we had, then, but one accompanied with real circles under the eyes, real lowered gradepoints, and real frayed nerves as well.

My last tale—dealing with the class setting as a real life encounter—concerns a joint seminar in mysticism which I was in with five students and three colleagues. We had been having quite a battle for a week over whether or not in a mystical experience the mystic in some sense transcends the Kantian categories of space and time. We went round and round without seeming to get anywhere. But then I heard that one of the students was sick and tired of talking about what the mystics *had* said or *might* say or *would* say on the matter, and was considering taking things into his own hands and actually "have it happen," right there is class. I was very well acquainted with the student and knew that what he had in mind was an LSD trip, through which he hoped some of his personal problems would be solved, in addition to the gaining of some insight into the nature of the mystical experience. After I pointed out to him, however, the probable consequences of publically taking a drug like LSD in an uncontrolled setting with no medical person present who was legally authorized to administer it to him, he grudgingly dropped the idea. But of course it was only by the merest chance that I had found out what he had in mind. (He later took the drug privately and had a "bad trip" which shook him to his very foundations.)

So here, now, we have another academic chamber of horrors, at least from most people's viewpoint, but it is quite different from the other one. Nothing wishy-washy about students wanting to expell other students for lack of commitment, nothing conformist about publically avowing homosexuality, nothing intellectually lacking in shooting down a prof's scholarship while citing him chapter and verse, nothing emotionally dead about dropping out of school and changing an entire life style, nothing uninvolved in having others you care for tear you apart by the demands they make on you, and nothing artificial about discussing mystical states while on an LSD trip right in class.

Now the problems involved in all of the above are obvious. What is not obvious at all is what to do about them. Here are four possible approaches.

First, perhaps the behavioral problems are the result of a mistaken idea of what education should be. Perhaps my ideal motives are really religious in nature and as such should be excluded from a non-religious setting. Indeed, about the only noncontroversial motive is the one involving intellectual commitment. However, if any of these motives are to be denied, part of the life's blood of teaching will be gone for me, so I will really need some convincing here.

Second, perhaps the solution is to re-educate the entire academic community so that it will consider the type of behavior under discussion acceptable and not view it as problematical at all. But most students would need as much re-educating as faculty and administrators, and to say the least one would be embarking upon an extremely ambitious program. In such a case I would also like to know what to do in the meantime, until a program like this could begin to bear fruit.

Third, perhaps the solution lies in training faculty to control situations better so that not as many problems arise. Graduate school preparation should possibly include training in group dynamics and some experience in teaching while under supervision. But again, changing graduate school curricula would be another very ambitious project and I would like some temporary guidelines to go by while this was being attempted.

Fourth, perhaps the thing to do is simply to stop looking for ideal solutions to un-ideal situations, to accept the problems that arise as the necessary and inevitable outcome of trying to do a decent job, and to give up trying to fight unrealistically the various academic "city halls."

In conclusion, it looks as if the present day faculty member may be condemned to "hear footsteps" of one variety or another. Either from below, from the minority of his students who simply can't stand the academic status quo, or from above, from the majority of his colleagues entrenched in the academic establishment who simply can't stand to give up this status quo. The ways in which this problem of "footsteps" is resolved may well control the shape of higher education for decades to come.

CLASSROOM BEHAVIOR AS A FUNCTION OF VALUE MOTIVATION

Editorial Comments

What Canning has attempted in his article is both to analyze behavior in the American college classroom in order to understand what underlying value-motivations actually produce this behavior, and also to present a theoretical set of ideal values to contrast with the real ones he discusses. (Using our earlier terminology, he is concerned with "facts" of value, along with a "theory of value.")

Viewing the academic environment as a *whole*, probably it would be granted that the confrontations occurring involve only a minority of students who could actually be considered dissenters. It might be fruitful, now, to investigate their value commitments and compare them with the value commitments of the educational establishment in general in an attempt to gain insight into the various confrontations that result. Canning has offered six basic values around which he feels many of the current controversies center and, while his approach in the article is exclusively classroom oriented, these six values would appear to have application to the entire educational environment as well.

First, he brings up the question of *a concern for truth*. Here, he feels, we have one of the key issues in many of the confrontations currently gripping our universities. Consider some of the following possible illustrations of this point. One, Black Student Unions across the country accuse predominantly white faculties of completely distorting or at least ignoring the truth concerning the black man's plight in this country, his culture, and his African origins. Two, Students for a Democratic Society accuse universities with ROTC departments of selling out to a propaganda arm of the military establishment concerned not with truth but with the white-washing of American foreign policy. And three, student dissenters in general often accuse alumni and boards of trustees of caring not at all for *truth*, but only for *success* in terms of lucrative research grants, impressive facilities, and graduates who "make it" in our competitive society. Confrontations over such explosive issues should hardly come as a surprise.

Second, he discusses the problem of *individuality* as it relates to the students of today. Consider the classroom situation, where the student who really has something to say often feels that he must remain silent, either out of fear of ridicule from his fellow students if they should happen to disapprove of his view, or out of fear of some form of subtle punishment from the professor who might not appreciate his genuine self-expression. Moving from the classroom to the dorm, the value conflict over individuality manifests itself in confrontation over the concept of "in loco parentis." Standards of behavior are sometimes imposed upon the students by university administrations when the students disagree violently with these standards, often disagreeing with the administration's right to set any standards at all. Moving beyond the campus altogether, the individuality issue comes up again in connection with the university's response to a student's political activity and possible encounters with law enforcement agencies as a result of this activity in the larger community outside the university. Over and over, the dissenters feel, the university shows its commitment to the conformist values of the herd, while they themselves think they are committed to the creative values of the individual. And thus new areas of confrontation continue to spring up all the time.

Third, he discusses the question of commitment to *intellectual rigor* as it bears on the educational situation. One possible application of this theme to an area of confrontation can be seen in the perennial conflict over "Mickey Mouse" courses on the one hand, and "Mickey Mouse" students on the other, with students and professors alike each accusing the other of lacking a real commitment to intellectual rigor. Another illustration could be found in the frustration of some students toward the oft-encountered "give them all the facts—cover all the ground" approach to education which seems to overlook an intellectually respectable analysis and critical evaluation of these facts. One other example of a conflict over the commitment to intellectual rigor concerns the "one-upmanship" that often goes on in the classroom situation, where either professor or students seem more interested in cleverly "scoring points" than in investigating the issue at hand in an intellectually honest way.

A fourth value mentioned which often seems at the heart of some of the conflicts encountered is *emotional openness*. Under this

heading would come conflicts over whether the professor should
stand behind his ego defense mechanism as well as his lecturn, in
dealing with his students in class. Some students continually push for
the professor to "come down off the mountain top" and share with
them *how he feels* as well as *what he thinks*. Of course, on the other
side of the isssue, we have the anxiety level of the students soaring
to great heights when a professor does decide to come down from
the mountain top and deal with them on a feeling level. This problem can be seen also in the academic community at large, in the
form of "role playing," where everyone attempts to "keep his cool,"
control his emotions, and in general "anesthetize" any "sticky"
situations that may come up. It is as if everyone checks his *feelings*
at the door upon entrance to the university and only brings his
mind with him to be engaged in the educational process. Some
cannot accept this, of course, and as a result an eventual confrontation can often be seen taking shape on the never-too-distant horizon.

A fifth value that Canning brought up as relevant to the understanding of what is really happening on the campuses today is that
of a *desire for community*. If this generation is truly the generation
of the "identity crisis," it does not do much good to have our
multiversities answer the question of "Who am I?" with "Your
student number is JLM-704-639-128." Some of the confrontations
that have occurred seem tied in with students' feelings of dehumanization at the hands of an impersonal bureaucratic system. The
students' IBM class cards (and the computers that process them)
would seem likely to continue to come in for destruction as long as
they offer such a fitting symbol for this impersonalization that the
students feel. Another example would relate to the unbearable
pressure that freshmen so often feel to "belong." This might help
to explain the "Go Greek," "Join a club," "Declare your major,"
"Get pinned," syndrome that seems to beckon to them. One other
example of frustration over a lack of community involves the cynicism sometimes felt by the "old timers" among the students, when
they decide that the ongoing "academic community" made up of
individual departments is really only an attractive myth, put forth
by the institutional propaganda machine to mask the true nature of
things: namely, a collection of independent fiefdoms, with some
professors committed to grinding out journal articles to enhance

their reputation, others to "signing up" students as majors to increase the size and power of their departments, and others yet committed to their research grants and only deigning to teach students as an unfortunately necessary evil. So the students drift about lacking a sense of community, until, that is, it dawns on them to join together with other frustrated drifters and make common cause against the enemy responsible for their condition. Thus the road to confrontation is found again.

The last value he discusses which seems to be involved in many of the conflicts erupting on our campuses today is that of *relevance*, as we see black students, over and over again, constantly pushing for anthropology courses in black culture, psychology courses in black identity, sociology courses in the black ghetto, and political science courses in techniques for black revolution. Some go further and push for black studies majors, black studies departments, and sometimes even separate colleges of black studies. The "lilywhite" curricula are not felt to be relevant to today's Blacks. Across the land, "free universities" are springing up, some even with substantial funding from the student bodies, in an attempt to offer courses that the students feel they really want and need. The curricula for such free universities are certainly not defined by self-perpetuating faculties on the basis of tradition, but by self-seeking students on the basis of relevance. A purusal of the courses offered in these programs would seem to give a clear indication as to where the real areas of relevance are. It might seem frustrating indeed, then, for a young man of today to sit in class busily plying his trade as student stenographer, frantically scribbling down all those very important facts, facts perhaps about problems that are not his, in a country that is not his, in an age that is not his, when his mind tends to wander to those rather more important facts that will face him upon graduation: soldiers must kill or be killed, draft resisters must go to jail or leave the country for good. Death, imprisonment, exile; no, there *is* some relevance. So again, it is small wonder that there is rebellion against such a system, a system that never seems able to get right down "to where it's at."

Canning suggests, then, that if our students of today could actually view the academic setting as one involving a real community of free individuals, truly committed to searching for those aspects of the truths that are relevant to them, in an intellectually honest and emotionally open manner, many areas of confrontation would begin to have creative resolution.

Now, we take a final look at the developing individual in his range of relationships as Switzer gives us a very definitive analysis of contemporary crisis theory relative to "changes in self-image, stated values, and behavior."

12

ON THE RECONSTRUCTION OF THE PERSON'S VALUE SYSTEM

Crisis as a Condition for Behavioral Change

DAVID K. SWITZER

Every developmental stage or major life decision has its stresses: the anxiety of giving up old patterns of responding, the threat of new responsibilities and situations calling for new forms of coping, new relationships with persons and new relationships between meanings, the creating of new meanings. A crisis is a problem situation which places these same demands upon the individual but which is compressed into a brief period of time. Caplan states: "The significance of a crisis is in its temporal telescoping of development" (2, p. 39). This is essentially the process which Starbuck has referred to in the crisis type conversion of adolescence. It is important to note that it is not just the difficulty of the situation as such, but its importance to the person, the degree of ego involvement, the amount of threat perceived, and how the person perceives the resources available to him to remove the threat in the learned expected time period. This brief transitional period has the power due to its emotional intensity to produce significant personality change. Again this seems to be what James referred to as the emotional excitement which had the power to produce character changes. Clinical evidence points toward the first six weeks of crisis as being vital in giving the direction (10). This personality change can be positive or negative, adding to or taking strength away from one's ego, depending upon whether new and effective means of coping have been developed or whether there has been behavioral decompensation.

There are four phases in the crisis situation:

1. There is the original rise in tension from the problem stimulus, the experience of anxiety, and perceived threat to the self. This calls forth the habitual problem-solving responses which have been learned previously and which might be generalized to this particular stimulus.

2. Because of the novelty of the situation and the continuing intensity of the stimulus, there is a lack of success in reducing the anxiety with the usual coping mechanisms in the period of time expected. A feeling of helplessness and ineffectualness results.

3. This is the "hitching up the belt" stage. The person delves more deeply into his reserve of strength and extends the range of his behavior in attempting to maintain his ego integrity. A redefinition of the problem may bring it into the range of prior experience. Trial and error behavior, both in thinking and in overt act, seeks to change or remove the problem stimulus. There may be a redefinition of one's role, thus a modification of identity. Active resignation may be integrated into the self image. The problem may be solved in this phase. If it is, the person usually becomes stronger, he moves farther along the continuum toward mental health, in that he has learned methods of dealing effectively with a new and threatening situation and has now brought this new learning into his repertoire of responses.

4. However, if the problem continues with no need satifaction, the tension produced by the anxiety may take the person beyond the threshold of rational responding, which is described by the term personality decompensation, where there are exaggerated distortions of one's identity or of the situation, rigid and compulsive ineffective behavior, socially

unacceptable behavior, extreme withdrawal, *et cetera* (10; 11, 141-142).

An extremely important factor to keep in mind is that a person usually does not face a crisis alone, and therefore he is either helped or hindered in his task of maintaining himself as a person by the other significant persons about him: family, friends, co-workers, members of the groups to which he belongs, professional workers of various kinds. Are these persons involved in the sufferer's life in such a way as to be giving psychosocial need satisfactions that compensate for the need frustration in other areas? Do they offer the opportunity for new decisions, new behavioral forms, new roles that are ego strengthening?

During a crisis, a person is more open to influence by others than he is any other time. His emotional equilibrium is upset, and even a relatively minor force will tip him to the side of resolution and strength or failure and its increased vulnerability. The presence of significant others may well have a major effect in determining his choice of coping mechanisms which in turn influence the outcome of the crisis. The most significant persons are those who are linked by the primary bonds of the basic need for love and who fit into his particular pattern of authority and dependency needs. The closer one is to these needs of the sufferer, the closer he actually is to the crisis, the more visible he is, the more likely he is to be called on by and have greater influence upon the person in need.

It can be seen that there are several assumptions in crisis theory. First, no matter what particular set of terms one uses to cast a theory of personality, there must be included some concept of the interpersonal development of the self; and that any loss of object with which one has identified one's self, or which one has introjected, or which has become a self-extension, is perceived and first responded to as a self-loss, a threat to the integrity of one's own ego. The maintenance and enhancement of one's self is seen as a function of one's relationship to others. The central value of every person's life is precisely the integrity of his own selfhood, and this corresponds with the central motivation of the enhancement or actualization of the self. Other forms of speech can be used to refer to this central motivation. Some, like Frankl (4), May (9), Lindgren (8), and others speak of the search for meaning. Allport declares that "the central nature of man is such that it presses toward a relative unification of life . . ." (1, p. 252).

We may also conceive of values in different terms as they reflect situational demands upon the organism, as stress is brought to bear, and as the individual under these demands seeks to strive toward and articulate his proximate goals in the service of maintenance and enhancement of the self. These proximate goals are not identical with this central motivation or even under certain conditions positively contributory to it in any long range or ultimate sense. Under stress, or under prior learning conditions of deprivation or overstimulation, they may be merely stopgap measures, protective or defensive behavior, which in long range terms are barriers to the fullest self-actualization or to high level unification.

The linking of value and motivation is done by Allport as he speaks of values as being "acquired preeminent motives" (1, p. 237). The tensions involved, and their impetus toward action are not the same as original, primitive motives, but are functionally autonomous. By this he means not that they are autonomous of one another nor unrelated to what has been taking place in the developing personality. To the contrary, they are "highly propriate"; i.e., well-anchored to the self. Indeed, to a large extent they constitute the self (1, p. 252). As a matter of fact, the self-structure of man demands the development of these additional motives for the continually expanding image of himself. The recognition and articulation of these are what we call values. These personal values, according to Allport, "are the dominating force in life, and all of a person's activity is directed toward the realization of his values" (1, p. 543).

Thus, to say that one's values are threatened is a way of speaking of the threat to a person's self-image, and vice versa. To participate with a person in crisis, that is, a time of threatened self-loss and the inability to draw immediately and easily from one's usual repertoire of responses the appropriate coping behavior, is also to participate in the reconstruction of that person's value system. This reconstruction involves not only the saving of one's selfhood, but through decision making and appropriate new behavior a person's self-valuation is increased and his repertoire of coping responses is expanded. In the successful resolution of crisis, the decisions and behavior which lead to new learning and the solving of the problem rather than decompensation are those which we term responsible.

That is, they produce human well-being, considering both one's self and others, and responsible behavior is seen as forming the foundation of sound interpersonal relationships. It is assumed that it is this type of conduct which we are concerned to produce.

What this paper is suggesting is that those who are concerned with the behavioral change of persons be prepared to capitalize upon and, in the best sense of the word, exploit the crises that every person undergoes, both developmental and accidental, and that we educate the total population insofar as possible to understand and be prepared to participate constructively in the crises of one another, both through planned and situational activity.

Crisis theory includes the observations concerning the centrality to the outcome of the crisis of the influence of other significant persons, significant either by already established relationship, by their role in the social structure, by their availability, or any combination of these. It is also to be noted that there is a "kairos," a specific, limited span of time in which other-person involvement is most crucial for the climactic learning of new coping behavior, involving the restoring of the self-image on the same or higher level, the experience of new personal strength, and in many instances the sense of a new valuation of life.

Practically every person alive at one time or another is in a position—by virtue of family relationship, job, voluntary group membership, or some other situation—to intervene in the crises of others, both developmental and accidental. Although we should not overlook the importance of intervention in the accidental crises, a major focus in regard to the matter of behavioral change should be on the developmental crises. Caplan referred to them. Others have developed the concept in a more detailed manner. Erikson speaks of developmental stages in terms of crisis "because incipient growth and awareness of a significant part-function goes together with a shift in instinctual energy and yet causes specific vulnerability in that part. . . . [Each step involves] a radical change in perspective. . . ." (3, p. 189). Each crisis is forced upon the maturing person by virtue of his existence as a person. Its inter- and intra-personal tasks must be accomplished in order to continue bringing the mature self into being, but each step carries with it inherent dangers.

Time is far passed when we should have begun to take seriously the possibilities of a massive assault on the positive resolution of these crises with the goal of attitudinal and value development and modification and the resulting change in personal conduct. This would involve several major points of attack.

The most crucial agency through which to work is that of the school. A comprehensive plan for the exploitation of crisis might be briefly outlined as follows:

(1) The programs of the schools themselves could be drastically reorganized to allow for the type of classroom procedure which involves pupils more fully in the educational process and which emphasizes a new quality of personal relationships within the class. Programs which have included small group procedures, self-teaching, and pupils teaching one another seem to give a direction in which to move.

(2) Necessary for this first suggestion is the requirement that all educators both study crisis theory and crisis intervention techniques and participate in encounter groups (or interaction groups or sensitivity training or whatever we might choose to call it) so that they may be more conscious of, and more prepared emotionally to participate in, the developmental and occasionally the accidental crises of the children and young people in their classes. Such encounter groups could be developed for all teachers presently practicing, in addition to their requirement in all teacher education programs.

(3) Encounter groups as such should be a part of the required curriculum of all schools, beginning perhaps with the sixth grade, continuing through high school graduation, and even through trade school, business school, and college. In these groups the crises surrounding the issues of relationships with parents, freeing one's self from parental ties, the search for values and meaning, sexual identity, vocational identity, preparation for marriage, and others could be dealt with at precisely the time they arise crucially for the student.

(4) Through the schools, parents can be urged to participate in discussion groups based on the model presented by

Hereford (5). In his study, data demonstrate that participation on the part of parents in only a limited number of non-professionally moderated discussion groups dealing with parent-child relationships produced statistically significant attitudinal and behavioral changes on the part of parents as measured by a written questionnaire and interview and behavioral changes on the part of their children as determined by peer-group selection and teacher ratings. These changes were in the direction of those assumed by the research team as being positively valued: namely, those of improved interpersonal relationships, less anxiety in relationship, greater self-determination, more effective decision making, more responsible behavior in relation to self and others. This is in keeping with both the assumptions and reported results of the rapidly expanding Parent Effectiveness Training courses developed by Gordon.

(5) Specific instruction on crisis therapy, crisis intervention techniques, and participation in basic encounter groups should be incorporated into the curriculum of all the helping professions (teaching, medicine, psychology, law, social work, youth organization leadership, ministry). In addition to the coverage given through the schools, the leaders of other children and youth organizations, church groups, social agencies, and clinics will also be keyed into participation in the developmental crises. Finally, all of those who work closely with adults in any context (educational, medical care, psychological and social services, the church) will be able to identify and intervene in the accidental crises of persons in such a way as to exploit these crises for the personal growth and ego strengthening of those persons, the reorientation of proximate values in the service of the ultimate value, the central motivation, that of the self-actualization of persons, which cannot be separated from the decisions for responsible behavior in relation to others.

This paper has sought to present contemporary crisis theory as a psychodynamic framework in which to understand occasions of high emotional stress when persons are most susceptible to changes in self-image, stated values, and behavior. In accidental crisis these changes may come about in a relatively brief period of time, perhaps six weeks or less.

The changes may be in the direction of the production of new coping behavior, added ego strength, heightened self-esteem, improved interpersonal relationships, and more responsible behavior. The central motivation for change corresponds with the central value for one's life, namely that of self-actualization, the source of all other stated proximate values.

Crucial in the crisis situation are interpersonal resources, key people who will intervene as agents of change with love and understanding, assistance in focusing on the source of the crisis and in the identification of intra- and interpersonal resources to overcome the crisis. The agents of change are members of family, voluntary group associations, and the various helping professions. The school is considered to be of central significance in the life of the child and young person because of the great amount of time spent in that context and because the school has certain access to the parents.

These helping professions and parents must be trained to be agents of change, both in an understanding of crisis theory and in the ability to intervene helpfully in both developmental and accidental crises. The method choice indicated in such training is that provided by basic encounter or other forms of group discussion method.

The result of such a program should be the maximum exploitation of both developmental and accidental crises, the intervention by helping persons in such a way that the motivation of self-actualization is allowed to bring about a higher level of integration and responsible behavior.

REFERENCES

1. Allport, Gordon, *Pattern and Growth in Personality*. New York: Holt, Rinehart & Winston, Inc., 1961.

2. Caplan, Gerald, *Principles of Preventive Psychiatry*. New York: Basic Books, Inc., Publishers, 1964.

3. Erikson, Erik, "Growth and Crises of the 'Healthy Personality,'" in *Personality in Nature, Society, and Culture,* eds. C. Kluckhohn and H. A. Murray. New York: Alfred A. Knopf, Inc., 1953.

4. Frankl, Viktor, *Man's Search for Meaning*. New York: Washington Square Press, 1963.

5. Hereford, Carl F., *Changing Parental Attitudes Through Group Discussion*. Austin: University of Texas Press, 1963.

6. James, William, *Varieties of Religious Experience*. New York: Longmans, Green & Co., 1902.

7. Klein, D. C. and Erich Lindemann, "Preventive-Intervention in Individual and Family Crisis Situations," in *Prevention of Mental Disorders in Children*, ed. Gerald Caplan. New York: Basic Books, Inc., Publishers, 1961.

8. Lindegren, Henry C., *Meaning: Antidote to Anxiety*. Camden, N. J.: Thomas Nelson & Sons, 1956.

9. May, Rollo, *Man's Search for Himself*. New York: W. W. Norton & Company, Inc., 1953.

10. Paul, Louis, "Crisis Intervention," *Mental Hygiene* (January 1966). See also, Morley, Wilbur E., "Treatment of the Patient in Crisis," *Western Medicine* (March 1965).

11. Starbuck, Edwin D., *The Psychology of Religion*. New York: Charles Scribner's Sons, 1900.

CRISIS AS A CONDITION FOR BEHAVIORAL CHANGE

Editorial Comments

It seems fitting to conclude the present series of articles with Switzer's for in it we see defined the full multidisciplinary approach. First, we find a *religious* valuation of man as both the *terminus a quo* and *terminus ad quem* of the undertaking as a whole. It is concern for the individual as a human being in crisis that constitutes the impetus for the investigation in the first place, and it is a desire to aid the individual in meeting his crises in a creative and self-actualizing way that provides the final end for the investigation. Both this concern and this desire can be seeen to be *religious* in nature. Second, *psychology* is seen to be the handmaiden to religion in this situation, for a developmental theory of personality is needed which will explain man's valuing process, as well as techniques of psychotherapy which will make it possible to help man deal successfully with the crises that he undergoes throughout different periods in his life. Clinical psychology in its theoretical role would attempt to furnish such a theory of personality, and in its applied role would attempt to furnish such techniques of psychotherapy. Third, the setting in which these crises are to be dealt with, on the basis of the types of theory and therapy just referred to, would be that of *education*. Thus, crises undergone by the individual during the educational process would be understood in terms of such a theory of personality, and treated in terms of such techniques of psychotherapy.

We can see, then, how an investigation such as Switzer's fully embodies the ideals of the multidisciplinary approach. Indeed, it is interesting to observe how his own background further illustrates these ideals. The concern for the worth of the individual which initially led him into the ministry, the professional training, both theoretical and applied, he received as a clinical psychologist, and the experience in education that his role as a dean has made possible, all contribute to his ability to carry out such multidisciplinary investigation in an uniquely qualified way.

Let us now return to education, viewed as one of our original areas of confrontation, to see some examples of how Switzer's proposal would be relevant to certain problems encountered here.

Utilizing Switzer's distinction betweeen developmental crises, which everyone undergoes necessarily as part of the maturing process, and accidental crises, which everyone undergoes only on occasion as the result of external factors entering into the life situation, we can see how many of the specific issues around which the current confrontations in education center are really a conjunction of both types of crises at once. Consider, for example, the typical garden-variety sort of "identity-crisis" that college seniors often undergo as they contemplate leaving the artificial but very secure womb created for them by the educational system. Everyone must face the problem of passing from adolescence to adulthood sometime, and in many Western societies the accompanying *"rites de passage"* are all tied in with commencement exercises from school. But just *who is it* who is commencing, and *what is it* that he is commencing upon? Thus the resulting identity crisis which is part of the developmental process.

Then, add to this some externally-induced crises and see how the problem is compounded a hundredfold. Take an emerging, but as yet not completely emerged, young adult and add to his woes by asking him to make an unusually crucial decision that only a fully mature adult could have any hope of making in a responsible manner. Ask a young black student in the United States what he plans to make of his life, and watch his anxiety level mount as the Black Militants stand ready to accuse him of "tomism" if he does not completely repudiate the values of the white majority, as the very same white majority stands ready to accept him (in its own limited way) if he will only commit himself to these values and compete successfully in terms of them, and as the Hippies stand ready to shower him with love if he will only but "do his own thing." Ask a Czech student what he plans to make of his life, and consider his response as troops of a foreign power patrol his campus, ready to snuff out any hints of "anti-Communist" activity, as student activists preach armed rebellion as the only way to restore their country's autonomy and self-respect, and as his national leaders exhort him to commit himself to the goals of the latter group but with methods that will not result in reprisals from the former group. Ask a young female student, now "liberated" by the pill, what she plans to make of her life, and attempt to understand her dilemma in deciding as she listens to the voices of tradition caution her from making pre-marital sex a part of her life while backing up their words with threats of punishment and guilt, as she listens to the voices against tradition hold these cautions in contempt while supporting their words with promises of pleasure and fulfillment, and as she listens to the voices of the new moralists exhort her to commit herself to a life motivated by neither fear of guilt nor desire for pleasure, but to one motivated by a responsible and aware but unconditioned love for others which would transcend both legalism and hedonism altogether. And lastly, ask a young male student in the United States who is facing the draft what he plans to make of his life, and then attempt to be empathetic with him in his anguish as he listens to those of "the right" speak to him of duty, honor, and patriotism while exhorting him to answer the call by "serving his country," as he listens to those of "the resistance" demand that he ignore the call and "serve mankind" instead, and as he listens to others yet who ask only that he "serve himself" by doing what he as an individual feels to be right, whatever it might turn out to be.

Developmental crises are inescapable for the student, then, since the problems involved in passing from adolescence to adulthood are endemic to the human situation. And when accidental crises are overlaid upon them, be they the result of sociological revolution, a foreign occupation, a medical breakthrough, or an agonizing war, it is small wonder that, as Switzer observes, the "time is far passed when we should have begun to take seriously the possibilities of a massive assault on the positive resolution of these crises . . ."

Switzer's idea for a program of crisis therapy embedded in the school system itself is an example of the type of proposal that needs *now* to be considered if ever the number of areas on the list of current confrontations is to be diminished.

Appendix

VALUES EXCERPTS

These quotations have been drawn from The Religion In Education Foundation Lexicon as relevant to the study of values. They are intended to be provocative in their points of view and kaleidoscopic in representation.

... anything that yields a satisfaction or provides a means for such satisfaction we designate a "value." Chronologically the viscerogenic or "bodily" values precede the psychogenic or "spiritual" values (p. 13). ... Our organisms are so constructed that our personal life is the highest value we ever know directly (p. 14). ... The world of art, the world of science, as well as the social universe around us, are all concerned with the production of values capable both of satisfying us and enlarging our horizon (p. 15).

> Gordon W. Allport, *The Individual and his Religion*. New York: The Macmillan Company, 1950.

A value or good is any conceivable object, person, event, process, or relationship, from the standpoint of its capacity to satisfy any particular interest and, therefore, as a means to life abundant or salvation in general.

Mordecai M. Kaplan, "The Need for Normative Unity in Higher Education," in *Goals for American Education,* eds. Lyman Bryson, Louis Finkelstein, and R. M. Maciver. New York: Harper & Row, Publishers, 1950, p. 313.

Value is that connection between enjoyable activities by which they support one another, enhance one another, and at a higher level, mean one another. At this higher level meaning may transform suffering and other forms of evil into experience of great value.

H. N. Wieman and R. W. Wieman, *Normative Psychology of Religion.* New York: Thomas Y. Crowell Company, 1935.

... in a very real sense one may say that our values are our motivations ... Values can be "carried around"; they become part of the person. When strong enough, they cannot be differentiated from the self; they are what makes up the self. And in any particular situation they play their part because the self plays its part. Since all behavior is interaction between an organism and an environment, values play their part in every behavior. One must know how much any one value has become a part of the self before one can judge to what extent it will condition the behavior in any specific situation where it is possible for that value to enter.

Bertha B. Friedman, *Foundations of the Measurement of Values,* New York: Teachers College, Columbia University Press, 1946, p. 2.

A value is the judgment of the quality of an experience ... The experiences that will gratify my needs create my values. Therefore, the structure and functioning of needs determine the range and limits of my values.

Ashley Montagu, *The Direction of Human Development.* New York: Harper & Row, Publishers, 1955, p. 307.

A thing—any thing—has value, or is valuable in the original and generic sense when it is the object of an interest—any interest. Or whatever is object of interest is ipso facto valuable. Value is thus defined in terms of interest, and its meaning thus depends on another definition, namely, a definition of interest. ... Interest is a train of events determined by expectation of its outcome. Or, a thing is an object of interest when its being expected induces actions looking to its realization or non-realization.

> Richard D. Brandt, *Value and Obligation: Systematic Readings in Ethics.* New York: Harcourt, Brace & World, Inc., 1961, p. 265.

It is widely recognized that one's "interests" change more often than one's "values." The reason, we believe, is to be found in the difference between the types of learning process involved. Just as the concept of attitude seems to be clarified by both the "canalization" and the "conditioning" processes, so the concept of "interest" rests on both processes. The relation of value to interest follows from the theoretical distinction made above between conditioning and canalization. Interests change rapidly as the mode of satisfying varies... Interests we suggest are conditioned stimuli pursued because of their relations to goal objects which are valued. Interests in turn are extinguished, as all other conditioned responses are extinguished, when the relations to the drives involved are destroyed.

> Gardner Murphy, *Personality: A Biosocial Approach to Origins and Structure.* New York: Harper & Row, Publishers, 1947, p. 283.

Value is a word of many meanings. To the scientist it connotes primarily truth. His values range along a true-false continuum. The artist's values are different. In some mysterious manner, they are measured in terms of aesthetic response. Value, for the moralist is a third kind of thing. Whatever it may be, it is evidently not mainly truth value nor aesthetic value, although it is certainly connected with these two.

> Thomas A. Cowan, "Social Interest and Value," in *Aspects of Value,* ed. Frederick C. Gruber. Philadelphia: University of Pennsylvania Press, 1959, pp. 59–60.

A value-system is a more or less consistent body of standards which gives meaning or direction to an attitude. An attitude, on the other hand, is an internal tendency to respond to an object. When the object becomes desirable, or when it is conceived as satisfying a wish or need, it becomes a value. In fine, attitudes and values are inseparable and together they form the attitude-value complex which guides an individual's behavior.

> Hubert Bonner, *Psychology of Personality.* New York: The Ronald Press Company, 1961, pp. 385–86.

Every society has a system of values—a set of interrelated ideas, concepts, and practices to which strong sentiments are attached. The word *value* as used here has the common sense meaning of something impor-

tant to the individual or group concerned. A value, then, is anything—
idea, belief, practice, thing—that is important to people for any reason.
Further, things can be important to us in a positive or a negative way—
we may put it that positive values are the things we are "for," while
negative values are the things we are "against" (p. 95).

Because the maintenance of the accepted values of a society is important and even to some degree necessary to its existence there is always
a set of positive and negative sanctions designed to support the established order. That is, there will be a patterned way by which approval
is expressed for those things having positive value to the society and
ways in which disapproval is expressed for those things having negative
value. . . . The positive sanctions in any society are usually less conspicuous than the negative ones but their role is no less important in
maintaining the value system. Human beings are dependent on their
fellows, and in every society men strive for the approval of their fellow-
men. The rewards come in status, prestige, power, recognition, and
privilege, as well as in more material ways. . . . Negative sanctions may
be social, legal, and magicoreligious or supernatural. The diffuse power
of public opinion expressed as scorn, contempt, or indifference is a
powerful means of social control. In a number of the simpler societies,
ridicule has been formalized as a satirical sanction . . . (pp. 110, 111).

Within all societies there are certain ritual or ceremonial patterns by
which values are collectively expressed and affirmed. These ritual procedures serve to create, strengthen, and transmit the sentiments necessary to the society's way of life. These practices can be understood
only if they are seen as symbolic procedures that operate in much the
same way as the idiomatic expressions of a language. As everyone
knows, idiomatic expressions make no sense when taken literally. They
simply have to be accepted as meaning what the people who speak the
language say they mean. There are in every society ritual practices that
can be understood only in this way. These expressive actions take
their meaning and value not from anything inherent in the acts themselves but from the emotions they evoke and the social contexts in
which they occur (p. 114).

> Ina Corinne Brown, *Understanding Other
> Cultures.* Englewood Cliffs, N. J.: Pren-
> tice-Hall, Inc., 1963.

The self is not merely a core of personality but also the center in one's
personal search for standards and ideals. Before adolescence begins,
some values and attitudes have been embraced by the child and pre-
adolescent. If emotions and sentiments are adequately developed, an
adolescent's response to externally embodied values will be magnified

during the later part of adolescence. Through repeated individualized responses to values and ideals as they are portrayed by his peers, parents, and community, an adolescent develops new traits and attitudes. New views and convictions are added when intellectual abilities are set into action in the total process of reality evaluation. There is common agreement among experts in the field that values, attitudes, and ideals act as prominent organizers of behavior as soon as an adolescent assimilates them. Through experience, the adolescent is able to bring his scale of values into focus and to set standards based on these values. He must, however, rely upon himself for this analysis so that he can properly evaluate his goals in life and ascertain the means necessary to obtain the goals.

...a primary source of information pertaining to the interpretation of meaning and values is the social environment of the adolescent. Values and meanings are "taken in" from significant persons such as parents, teachers, and peer-group leaders. Peers begin to rank high as an adolescent moves to free himself from parental and adult influence. Occasionally, life-determining decisions are the results of intimate friendships. In the advanced years of adolescence, societal and cultural norms and expectations gain substantially in their conditioning power.

Late adolescence is an age during which the formulation of a value scale often becomes final. Many adolescent difficulties can be traced to the fact that our society has not set norms of values. As a result, the adolescent is unable to understand the importance and place of religious and moral values and activate them in his own plan of growth and adjustment. More than occasionally the ultimate source of value and sanction remains unidentified.

Justin Pikunas and Eugene J. Albrecht, *Psychology of Human Development.* New York: McGraw-Hill Book Company, 1961, pp. 217–18.

Man is a natural being with a fixed core, directed toward a good which is pertinent to all that exists. He has infinite value because he has infinite responsibility.

Paul Weiss, *Nature and Man.* New York: Holt, Rinehart & Winston, Inc., 1947, p. 267.

Whether any scientist likes to admit it or not, any interpretation he makes must be regarded as a value judgment. ... Scientific research itself has demonstrated that the scientist's own value judgments are involved in scientific inquiry from beginning to end (p. 6).

"Objectivity," as it is usually conceived, is not only illusory—it is undersirable. Any scientific data become inert and meaningless without value judgments, and science is reduced to a routine collection of facts (p. 7).

Because scientific inquiry is permeated with value judgments, no scientist can avoid some responsibility for the judgments he makes. ...Because value judgments do play so important a role in scientific thinking, every effort must be made to discover ways and means of making value judgments themselves the subject matter for scientific inquiry (p. 8).

An outstanding characteristic of man is his capacity to sense the value in the quality of his experience. The value man is able to sense in the quality of his experience we will call the "value attribute" of experience. This experienced value attribute is a pervasive and inseparable aspect of every experience. All human wants, urges, desires, and aspirations are permeated with some value attribute (p. 23).

Man tries to recapture qualities he has experienced on previous occasions: in his social gatherings, his ways of satisfying physical needs, his esthetic experiences, his work, or his play. He wants to recapture these experiences simply because he enjoys experiencing the value attribute related to them (p. 25).

The value attribute that pervades every experience is a crucially important fact. It is the catalyzer needed to produce nearly all of our actions...We remember the values experienced in life and we store them up, building out of them a standard or pattern of values which we inevitably, though generally unconsciously, use for later reference. Against the pattern of values derived from past experiences, we sense the quality of our present experience. It is the only value standard we know. On the basis of our acquired system of values we characterize our present experiences variously as "worthwhile," "satisfying," "pleasant," "fruitless," "disappointing," and the like.

It is in terms of experience that the "worthwhileness" of an action is tested. The value of the quality in experience comes into being only in concrete situations. In general it is not subject to recall as are conceptual abstractions...if no value attribute in action is experienced, there is no participation in the on-going process of living and growing (p. 26–27).

...Sensed value attributes characterize all man's experience. Whitehead was referring to this characteristic of man when he wrote that "the ultimate motive power, alike in science, in morality, and in religion, is the sense of value, the sense of importance. It takes the various forms of wonder, of curiosity, of reverence, of worship, of tumultuous desire for merging personality in something beyond itself. This sense of value imposes on life incredible labors, and apart from it life sinks back into the passivity of its lower types." The word "value," Whitehead has explained, "is the word I use for the intrinsic reality of an event" (pp. 27–28).

> Hadley Cantril, *The "Why" of Man's Experience*. New York: The Macmillan Company, 1950.

Value theory is receiving increasing attention from students of the behavioral sciences but the forms in which this theory is being developed exhibit two major deficiencies. One of these is the failure to recognize that there is no *single problem of value* but rather a congeries of problems referred to as the problem of value. In the existing literature the term "value" is used pluralistically for a variety of contexts and objectives, with no common semantic or syntactical referent. This makes for a good deal of faulty communication in which people talk past one another because of the intellectual excitement over a common term. . . .The second misfortune is that there is an increasing tendency to treat values as abstractions, to analyze situations of value *structurally*, using the apparatus of logic and mathematics, and thereby to treat the attribute of value as inherent in things or contexts, disengaged from evaluators (p. 175).

Education in the Western world, whether of the school, the church, the home, the institution, or the occupation, fails to deal with values in the only significant way with which they can be dealt. Our educational forms fail to spell out the human contexts to which a held value is relevant, whether these contexts involve our intimate attachments to single persons or the more impersonal relationships to larger groups. Even more they fail to spell out the archetypal situations, simple or complex, to which our values are germane. To do this properly the exercise of imagination is required. One has to learn to reproduce sympathetically, as it were, those phenomenal fields of other individuals in which conflicts and uncertainties of a given sort could arise, and which could demand for their resolution any one of some appropriate set of values. No large body of educators is today dedicated to this sympathetic training of the imagination and to enhancement of the awareness of psychic individuality, the phenomenally different value orientations from which so many fundamental differences in behavior emerge (p. 178).

As a result of the loss of authenticity in the expression of value, modern man possesses no genuine intentional anchors in life (p. 179).

Values cannot be solely intellectual matters. Feeling is a very necessary accompaniment to them. Feeling seems to be an accompaniment of proximity and shared experience, imitation followed by the genuine appearance of the emotion simulated, understanding coupled with good will, and similar social accidents. However, the problem of generating the feeling tone which is appropriate to an abstract value, is still pretty much unsolved. Unless such appropriate feeling accompanies the verbal expression of our values and education supplies a rough notion of the contexts which call for the enactment of these values, they will continue to remain abstractions (p. 181).

> Henry Winthrop, "Phenomenological and Existential Considerations Surrounding the Problem of Value," *Journal of Existential Psychiatry* (Fall 1961).

We define the value potential as the range of values an individual is able to encompass, in terms of *awareness, appreciation, acceptance,* and *activation.* By "ability" we mean a functional aptitude, determined by innate potentials as well as by experience and learning as by emotional and motivational development.

A person's value potential may be comprehensive or limited, depending on the individual's own basic tendencies, on what has been brought to his attention during his lifetime, and on the degree of freedom of action that his emotional balance permits.

The value potential is then a *function* of the innate and experientially developed structure of a person's basic tendencies. An individual whose basic tendencies show a good equilibrium and are well integrated has the greatest value potential.... An individual whose basic tendencies are in disequilibrium and not integrated has a limited value potential, because of an exclusive or predominant tendency in one or the other direction.

Of course we have to appreciate the fact that in most individuals there exists a hierarchical order as far as their values are concerned, whether they know this or not. But in the well-adjusted person whose basic tendencies are in equilibrium, there is no rigidity regarding this hierarchy.

> Charlotte Buhler, "Considerations about the Role of Values and Beliefs in Human Life," *Journal of Existential Psychiatry* (Fall 1961), p. 168.

Identity is a coherent sense of self. It depends upon the awareness that one's endeavors and one's life make sense, that they are meaningful in the context in which life is lived. It depends also upon stable values, and upon the conviction that one's actions and values are harmoniously related. It is a sense of wholeness, of integration, of knowing what is right and what is wrong and of being able to choose (p. 19).

Values determine goals, and goals define identity. The problem of identity, therefore, is secondary to some basic trouble about value. The existence of such trouble is generally recognized and it is considered an urgent problem of our time. Scientists, however, have been inclined to sidestep it. Wishing to keep the field of empirical work uncluttered, they have usually relegated such problems to moralists and philosophers. This position is becoming untenable. If the scientist restricts his interest and responsibility to the laboratory, it will fall to the lot of others to determine the value of his findings and the ends they are to serve. And, in fact, the "others" will not usually be moralists and philosophers but men of action (p. 174).

Values are structured in a hierarchy. Different orders of values, therefore, require different treatment (p. 175).

Values are the products of the life process and are coextensive with this process. They do not exist in a void, but are engendered by the activities of men. No values transcend man in origin, though many transcend the evidence at hand. The belief in God goes beyond scientific knowledge, but it does not go beyond man. It is a product of man's religious, ceremonial, and myth-making activities. Transcendental values, therefore, like all other values, arise from and are perpetuated by the activities of men. . . . Value is a product of sustained and purposeful activity, rather than casual and random activity. . . . Value is a product, not only of activity, but also of choice. We do not value all things that we deal with and produce. Certain things or conditions or experiences are seen as "better than" certain others. This perception and decision are essential to the emergence of values (p. 177).

The values which derive from tool-using retain the characteristics of the instrumental process, and the values which derive from myth-making retain the characteristics of the institutional process (p. 178).

> Allen Wheelis, *The Quest for Identity.*
> New York: W.W. Norton & Company,
> Inc., 1958.

. . . a value is a joint-product of man's nature and of the world in which he lives. There are no values independent of man, but there are value-possibilites in his nature and in the world whose realization awaits his criticized and marshalled efforts. Man does not make his own basic nature, and he is not responsible for the possibilities of value in the world beyond him. The values he does approve and realize must therefore, be taken as testimony to the fact that man's criticized wants and the constitution of the world do not work at cross-purposes.

Peter A. Bertocci, *An Introduction to the Philosophy of Religion.* Englewood Cliffs, N.J.: Prentice-Hall, Inc., 1951, p. 350.

... modern man has to a great extent lost the power to affirm and believe in *any* value. No matter how important the content of the values may be, or how suitable this or that value may be on paper, what the individual needs is a prior capacity, namely, *the power to do the valuing.* The triumph of barbarism in such movements as Hitlerian fascism did not occur because people "forgot" the ethical traditions of our society as one might misplace a code. The humanistic values of liberty and the greatest good for the greatest number, the Hebrew-Christian values of community and love for the stranger were still in the textbooks, were still taught in Sunday School, and no archeological expedition was needed to unearth them. People rather have lost ... the inner capacity to *affirm*, to experience values and goals as real and powerful for themselves.

In actual life the real value is something we experience as connected with the reality of our activity, and any verbal discussion is on a quite secondary level ... unless the individual himself can affirm the value; unless his own inner motives, his own ethical awareness, are made the starting place, no discussion of values will make much real difference. Ethical judgment and decision must be rooted in the individual's own power to evaluate. Only as he himself affirms, on all levels of himself, a way of acting as part of the way he sees reality and chooses to relate to it—only thus will the value have effectiveness and cogency for his own living. For this obviously is the only way he can or will take responsibility for his action. And it is the only way that he will *learn* from his action how better to act next time, for when we act by rote or rule we close our eyes to the nuances, the new possibilities, the unique ways in which every situation is different from every other. Furthermore, it is only as the person chooses the action, affirms the goal in his own awareness, that his action will have conviction and power, for only then will he really believe in what he is doing.

Rollo May, *Man's Search for Himself.* New York.: W.W. Norton & Company, Inc., 1952, pp. 216–17.

... man is a value affirming, a value cherishing, and a value realizing animal. He finds, therefore, value judgments to be essential, which means also that moral judgments based on some more or less adequate knowledge are integral to his living. The conscious identification of values thus becomes an imperative assignment, initially; and some basis for weighing and choosing among values is required ultimately. Also, the processes by which values are striven for through conscious effort cannot be ignored, nor can we fail to realize that for these values to have directive influence over conduct, they must have an appeal and an outcome which are clearly found to be desirable and satisfying to the individuals involved (p. 121).

... we have in historic experience built into the ideal meaning of certain concepts a nucleus of values which as a society we strive continuously to make influential. In our American society, some of the most important of these concepts, symbolized and summarized in words, have come to identify widely shared values. I refer to such words as democracy, freedom, love, science, rationality, leadership, personality, community, creative art, cultural pluralism, and world organization.

The mere mention of these concepts suggests that if they are to be realized, they have to be understood in their operating, know-how phases. The grasping of the "executive" or operative ways and means of better living thus becomes one crucial assignment of higher education. And if such values as these are to be controlling, individuals have to be literally *possessed by them*, so that they will be effective in action and satisfying in outcome.

If values are to be known as good, and if they are to be truly learned, they have to be lived, expressed, and found desirable. This experiencing of values helps substantially to define the role of higher education, for its role is designed to interpret these symbols operationally and enthusiastically to enhance their necessary contribution to individual and social living. Education exists, I repeat, to bring each person into an awareness of and participation in the realizing of the best of these humanly prized, historically tested aspirations and activities (p. 122).

> Ordway Tead, "Religion in Municipal Colleges," in *American Education and Religion*, ed. F. Ernest Johnson. New York: Harper & Row, Publishers, 1952.

Personal values are the dominating force in life, and all of a person's activity is directed toward the realization of his values.

> Gordon W. Allport, *Pattern and Growth in Personality*. New York: Holt, Rinehart & Winston, Inc., 1963, p. 543.

If meanings and values were just something emerging from the subject himself—that is to say, if they were not something that stems from a sphere beyond man and above man—they would instantly lose their demanding force. They could no longer be a real challenge to man, they would never be able to summon him up, to call him forth.

Viktor E. Frankl, "Dynamics, Existence and Values," *Journal of Existential Psychiatry* (Summer 1961), pp. 9–10.

In every society, men strive for whatever they judge to be good and right. What men strive for must be worth the physical and psychological endeavor entailed in the struggle.

The concept of value is important for it replaces the needs approach to motivation with a positive explanation of why men do what they do. In the needs theory, good is equated with the elimination of a lack. A man strives for love because he does not have it and needs it. Essentially he is struggling to fill a void. The introduction of the idea of value, however, changes this interpretation of man's struggle for love to a striving for something that he has learned is good and right or has value. This substitution of value for needs supplies a positive rationale for motivation where formerly there was only a negative one.

Essentially a value is a learned belief so thoroughly internalized that it colors the actions and thoughts of the individual and produces a strong emotional-intellectual response when anything runs counter to it...

Values are learned. Infants do not come into the world equipped with the knowledge that some behaviors and thoughts are "good" or "right." Adults begin teaching values explicitly the day a child is born and reinforce learning through a never-ending system of rewards and punishments...

The child first learns values from the important adults in his life, especially his parents. Later, school personnel and his peers take over some of this teaching function with the peer group assuming major importance. As the youngster moves through adolescence, association with people of differing values leads the youngster to examine his own and modify or reinforce them in the light of his experiences. The process of value modification or value reinforcement is lifelong for the individual as his horizons widen and his experiences increase.

Ruth Barry and Beverly Wolf, *Motives, Values and Realities: A Framework for Counseling.* New York: Teachers College, Columbia University Press, 1965, pp. 39–41.

... it is only as a person that an individual can use concepts or engage in any sort of ideal and symbolic form of activity. On the other hand, it is only through the development of his native capacity for these that he can achieve personality. Since his individual needs must be satisfied through the culture, the ends he seeks and the means he uses must either be formulated in cultural terms or, as implicit in the culture, be expressible through its language. The values around which his personality is organized must attach to something objective and as such have a conceptually determinable place in the culture. On the other hand, it is the development of what we have loosely called generalized habits and of the "idealized" modes of feeling involved in such habits that makes it possible for the person to engage in the fully ideal activity of thought. Thus, there is a correspondence and mutual dependence between what we may call the emotional and intellectual organization which constitutes personality.

. . . a highly complex society like our own, itself poorly integrated and with a great variety of institutions in process of rapid development, makes great and often conflicting demands on individuals. It stimulates the development of complex personalities but provides no simple basic framework of accepted values within which they may be organized. Moreover, since our culture is both highly literate and conceptually articulate, it becomes important, especially for individuals who participate deeply in the culture, to reach an inner adjustment at a conscious and conceptual level. The very function of conceptual thought may become transformed under such conditions and take on a deeper and more vital importance for human life. On a basis of unformulated beliefs and unquestioned values, the ordering of personal life becomes impossible; it must rest upon a conscious reformulation and critical appraisal of ideas and values. We must not forget, however, that such an achievement is no mere intellectual feat of constructing a theoretical system of abstract concepts. Critical appraisal must proceed from a value matrix implicitly in the culture and appropriated to new uses by the individual.

Grace A. de Laguna, *Existence and the Human World*. New Haven: Yale University Press, 1966, pp. 208–10.

The motive, please note, is postulated and not observed. . . . There are many words to label this inner determination: *purpose, intent, aim, goal, decision.* We say, "my mind is made up," "I am set to act," "I intend to do this." To the psychologist this presents a problem, or better, a group of problems. A postulated motive has various attributes. It persists in time. It directs and regulates behavior. It is terminated by the achievement of an end or goal. It energizes and arouses action in the individual. A motive, moreover, can be latent (inactive) for considerable periods of time. . . . Motives are described in words, and they may also be inferred from overt behavior. . . The layman commonly distinguishes between motives and habits. The difference is this: a motive is properly described as a readiness to carry out some specific act. The motive is capable of building up tension or causing action. The motive, moreover, is removed by completion of an intended act, i.e., by a goal response. A habit, contrastingly, lacks these attributes. Habits are patterns of neutral organization that make it possible for individuals to carry out innumerable acts of skill; but they do not instigate, sustain, and regulate action in a dynamic sense. Insofar as they do, they are motivating.

> Paul Thomas Young, *Motivation and Emotion: A Survey of the Determinants of Human and Animal Activity*. New York: John Wiley & Sons, Inc., 1961, pp. 6–7.

Knowledge is actually thought to be capable of some mysterious internal combustion that gives it dynamic. In spite of Dewey's life-time devotion to the proof of its instrumental nature, many—without intending to renounce Dewey—still cling to the notion that ideas are self-propagating. Knowledge is but the rudder of the ship; motive is the engine. Knowledge gives *direction* to our desires. It indicates the means by which those desires may be brought to realization.

Yet how widespread, how subtle, how disastrous is the belief that knowledge about right produces a tendency to do right. This superstition is as old as human thought. Because the things we know are so much more vivid in our thought than the urge we feel, it seems as though the knowledge caused the action. This illusion is reinforced by generations of training to accept confidently this assumption implicit in all discussions and explanations of conduct. . . . Until we distinguish between ideas and the motives that are associated with them we shall continue to waste time and energy in imparting correct ideas, neglecting the building up of the necessary motives as accompaniments; and those unmotivated ideas will continue sterile. *Knowledge about* the right does not produce right conduct.

. . . The task of motivation is not merely to find inducements and attach them to momentary choices. If adequate motives cannot be found, they must be created. Especially must they be created in anticipation of future need (pp. 9-14). Likes and dislikes are *motives*. The control of motives is the control of likes and dislikes. It is not the control of knowledge or skill or reasoning. The *means* of securing what one likes and escaping what one dislikes are intellectual patterns. Motives deal with the feeling tone connected to those images. Intellectual processes deal with sense images; affective processes relate to the field of satisfaction and annoyance. . . . In a voluntary choice a motive is one's feeling of liking or disliking the outcome pictured. The intellectual processes of skill, memory, imagination, and reasoning are means by which he brings to pass the outcomes which he most strongly desires.

. . . Every adjustment that one makes involves stimulation from some sense organ, immediate or recalled, whose meaning awakens some degree of satisfaction or annoyance . . . Some motive is present whenever a change is undertaken, whether the act is carried out normally or thwarted. It is of the utmost importance to note this fact because, in analyzing emotion, the relation of satisfaction and annoyance (known as affective states) to the total experience is highly significant (pp. 33-40).

> Harold Saxe Tuttle, *How Motives are Educated*. Ann Arbor, Michigan: Edward Bros., Inc., 1941.

For society to remain alive, it must feed on emotion. For an individual to remain happy, and even alive, maybe, he must hold some unrational or unrationally intense belief. If we are to use the pragmatic criterion according to which a belief is true if it helps the organism to maintain itself efficiently, then many at least superficially incompatible beliefs can be true, though perhaps unequally true, or one can be true at one time or for one person, and another at another time or for another person. It might be less confusing to say that the impulse to believe is such that it must accept the truth of some of its objects, which are therefore true so far as the person at the moment is concerned.

The pragmatic criterion of truth need not be accepted, or may be interpreted otherwise, but that does not change the basic point, which is that we are subject to a nearly irresistible need to believe. The need we can escape only insofar as we can avoid infancy and childhood, a detour too extravagant for most of us to make, and insofar as we can discover utterly objective guiding truths and values, a discovery the merely human among us find too difficult to accomplish. The dissipation of guilt is not an intellectual process. Ambition, devotion, love, and hatred, are not intellectual. Of the many illusions to which reason is subject, one of the most persistent and endangering is the illusion that it is the master. Reason is only the luminous tip of a massive and impulsive subterranean psyche. If it is to make the best of the powers it has and cast its light back into the dim psyche out of which it has emerged, it must make of itself a humiliated light. It may humiliate reason to acknowledge that it must serve irrational desires, discipline itself in the permissive prohibitions of ritual, and sustain itself with faith. But to refuse to acknowledge its needs would be still more humiliating, because it would be an avowal that reason could not even see, much less govern, its nature.

Mortimer Ostow and Ben-Ami Scharf-stein, *The Need to Believe*. New York: International Universities Press, 1954, p. 159.

The experimental mind . . . believes that values evolve within the course of ordinary experience. They have a natural basis and origin because man is a creature of interests, and he has to react selectively to his surroundings in order to maintain these life interests. Men become intelligent about values as they become intelligent about their actions—about the conditions upon which they depend, about the consequences to which they lead. As Dewey has emphasized, not all of the things that are immediately liked are likeable, or are all of the things that men desire really desirable. The difference between the merely "desired" and that which is counted "desirable" is the difference between impulsive acts, and those acts whose conditions and consequences have been inspected, evaluated, and judged to be good. The latter activities are considered desirable or valuable not simply because of their immediately prized qualities, but because they are judged to harmonize with other valued interests and to "lead-on" in such a way as to expand, not contract, the totality of significant experience, meaning and activity.

For the mind nurtured in experimental practices, morals and values do not constitute a separate realm and subject-matter. Since consequences cannot be separated from conditions, judgments about values cannot be divorced from judgments about facts. A human being can make an intelligent manifestation of preference only as he has knowledge of the concrete conditions that are involved in his various activities. The child who is learning through empirical procedures to discriminate the better from the worse in the different mundane spheres of human activity is, at the same time, growing in capacity for moral judgment. It is in and through these varied and interrelated life activities that the real occasions for moral decision arise, and the child grows in his capacity to function as a responsible moral agent as he grows in his ability to make judgments of the good and the bad in terms of concrete consequences. Moral behavior is thus a function of the entire experience of the child, and all education is inescapably a form of character education.

John L. Childs, *Education and Morals*. New York: Appleton-Century-Crofts, 1950, pp. 166-67.

. . . there is a "natural" period of uprootedness in human life: adolescence. Like a trapeze artist, the young person in the middle of vigorous motion must let go of his safe hold on childhood and reach out for a firm grasp on adulthood, depending for a breathless interval on a relatedness between the past and the future, and on the reliability of those he must let go of, and those who will "receive" him. Whatever combination of drives and defenses, of sublimations and capacities has emerged from the young individual's childhood must now make sense in view of his concrete opportunities in work and in love; what the individual has learned to see in himself must now coincide with the expectations and recognitions which others bestow on him; whatever values have become meaningful to him must now match universal significance.

Identity formation thus goes beyond the process of *identifying* oneself with others in the one-way fashion described in earlier psychoanalysis. It is a process based on a heightened cognitive and emotional capacity to *let oneself be identified* as a circumscribed individual in relation to a predictable universe which transcends the circumstances of childhood. Identity thus is not the sum of childhood identifications, but rather a new combination of old and new identification fragments. For this very reason societies *confirm* an individual at this time in all kinds of ideological frameworks and assign roles and tasks to him in which he can *recognize* himself and *feel recognized*. Ritual confirmations, initiations, and indoctrinations only enhance an indispensable process by which healthy societies bestow traditional strength on the new generation and thereby bind to themselves the strength of youth. Societies thus verify the new individual and are themselves historically verified, for the individual is induced to put at the disposal of societal processes that "conflict-free" energy which he was able to save up, as it were, from his infantile conflicts. Such an intricate process, however, which has evolved both with the evolution of the individual and of society cannot be fostered by synthetic values, nor can the product be confirmed with empty ceremony: here the weakened creeds of the West and the manufactured ideologies of the Communist world may meet a common obstacle.

Erik H. Erikson, *Insight and Responsibility*. New York: W. W. Norton & Company, Inc., 1964, pp. 90-91.

Value implies a code or standard which has some persistence through time, or more broadly, which organizes a system of action. Value, conveniently and in accordance with the cultural usage, places things, acts, ways of behaving, goals of action on the approval-disapproval continuum. What we want and what we value are separated in the world of experience, writes Kluckhohn.

Values involve appraisal in terms of some standard in addition to and over the immediately given, the immediately energizing and directing motivational determinants; or for that matter, in terms of some standard dominant over any desired anticipations. Value determines what we ought to do, not what one necessarily desires to do. Sometimes "wants" and "desires" are identical with "oughts!" Kluckhohn states, however, that cathexis (impulse) and value seldom coincide completely. Cathexis is generally a short term and narrow response, whereas value implies a broader and long-term point of view. A value restrains impulses, or canalizes them in terms of wider and more enduring goals . . .

Values are operative when an individual selects one line of action, or thought, over another to the degree that the selection is influenced by generalized codes rather than determined simply by impulse or temporary expediency. The selection is not necessarily at the level of awareness of the individual involved in the selection. It simply happens; but the generalized codes may be operating. Not only the goal but the way of carrying out a valued goal can be evaluated. There is no wrong way to obtain a right goal, provided that values are operating in both the choice of goals and *also in the modes of attainment.*

> Dorothy Rethlingshafer, *Motivation as Related to Personality.* New York: Mc-Graw-Hill Book Company, 1963, pp. 266–67. Insert 25, *Social Values,* adapted from C. Kluckhohn, *Values and Value-Orientation,* in *Toward a General Theory of Action,* eds. Talcott Parsons and Edward A. Shils. Cambridge, Mass.: Harvard University Press, 1951, pp. 339, 399.

In directing the "human enterprise" then, man must not only acquire information about himself and his world and develop the competencies for dealing with his problems, but he must also come to grips with the problem of value—of what is good for him and what is not—and ultimately with the problem of the meaning of his existence—of just what his role in the universe is. For our purposes, we may think of these problems in terms of two simple categories: "know-how" and "know-why."

The Problem of "Know-How." To direct his behavior effectively, man must first of all acquire information about himself and his world. He must learn about his needs, his potentialities, his rational and irrational tendencies, and the many other facets of his nature which enable him to fill in a realistic self-picture. Man must also learn about the world in which he lives—not only the inanimate world, but the world of plants and animals and human groups. He must learn about its dangers, its potentialities for meeting his needs, and the principles inherent in its operation—information that will enable him to understand his world and to some extent control it.

Man's views of himself and his world, whether accurate or inaccurate, are primary determiners of his behavior. For the goals he strives after and the means he selects for trying to achieve them are largely determined by what he conceives himself to be, by what he conceives himself able to become, and by the way he pictures the opportunities and limitations of the world around him. People who view human nature as basically kind and good are likely to behave in different ways from those who view human nature as basically cruel and selfish. Similarly, people who view their environment as hostile and dangerous are likely to behave differently from those who view it as friendly and full of opportunity.

In addition to acquiring information about himself and his world, man must also acquire the competencies requisite for getting along in human society and for carrying out his individual purposes . . .

The Problem of "Know-Why." Achieving effective adjustment is not simply a matter of acquiring information and developing necessary competencies. Man must also solve the problem of "know-why"—he must find a comprehensive value system to give him a sense of purpose and to guide his adjustive behavior in specific situations. From among the many goals, means, and ways of living that are available to him, he must choose those he thinks will best meet his needs. His choices are inevitably based upon his assumptions or judgments concerning value— upon what he thinks is right and will lead to his greatest satisfaction and well-being . . .

In his pursuit of values, man is inescapably confronted with the problem of *meaning*—with the question of what life is all about. This concern with meaning, so basic to human thought and action, is unique to man.

> James C. Coleman, *Personality Dynamics and Effective Behavior*. Glenview, Ill. Scott, Foresman and Company, 1960, pp. 6-8.

In the positive view of mental health, individual and interhuman values are not at odds. The individual who truly loves himself cannot destroy others or hurt them without destroying himself. He can only love others as he does himself. The individual who flourishes as a truly creative person enhances his personal life and in turn creates social values and social health; that is, he frees others to be themselves and to develop their potentialities. The creative person is not interested in changing others, as such, but only in expressing what he must express in accordance with his intrinsic nature and his experience. Though he is not motivated to influence others, through his own creativity he enables others to trust their own perceptions.

Man who is at one with the world has a basic urge to develop and realize himself and through himself to enrich the world. This is the basis for the development of all ethical values. The person's striving to express his creativity is the positive and healthy essence of personality. Different individuals may express this in different ways, in variations and unique patterns; but the presence of such intrinsic creativity is the incomparable given of all human nature.

In the American society the individual often gropes with two aspects of a basic conflict: the struggle to become a self-fulfilling person, and the need for social recognition and approval. While every person wants to be accepted and valued, the threat of ostracism and rejection often forces the individual away from truly creative expression which is necessary for his own personal growth. Many persons fail to remain free and develop true self-insight when forced to respond to social demands and to others, at the expense of their own self-responsiveness.

> Clark Moustakas and David Smillie, "The Significance of Individual Creativity for Psychotherapy," *Journal of Individual Psychology* (Nov. 1957), 13, pp. 160-61.

Concern with moral and spiritual values represents a high point in the development of the self-concept. In general, older adolescents are more concerned about the destiny of man and the meaning of life than are younger boys and girls. Religion emphasizes love, faith, and hope. In a sense, moral and spiritual values are basic to self-esteem, for without hope for the future, it does not matter much what one becomes. Some system of beliefs which gives meaning to life is characteristic of the mature personality. The ultimate in self-realization involves love for something outside and beyond the self.

> Ruth Stang, *The Adolescent Views Himself*. New York: McGraw-Hill Book Company, 1957.

Destructiveness of attitude and behavior is nurtured and strengthened during the course of faulty upbringing of a child in his family and through influences in his neighborhood. The psychiatrist can rethink his position on the causes of crime, delinquency, and other forms of antisocial behavior and question the assumption of relating antisocial behavior mostly to mental illness or extremes of poverty, rather than to the absence of, or to faulty value education. If religious, social, and moral values are not presented to children in their formative years, then they most likely will lack them.

Conscience is recognized by most authorities as representing inner controls. Although the capacity for conscience is innate, and there are dimensions of conscience that extend beyond mere socialization, much of the content and application of conscience come from the family and society. Thus, the child needs to be introduced to the higher value system of the group in which he is living. Where instruction is not given, or where the family and society have become uncertain of basic values and consequently have developed a collective instability and uncertainty about values, one sees a developmental defect in the spiritual and moral dimension of man.

> James A. Knight, *A Psychiatrist Looks at Religion and Health.* Nashville, Tenn. Abingdon Press, 1964, p. 200.

As I conceive it, religion roots in the most general cultural orientations of human action—orientations which underlie the structuring both of social systems and of the personalities of individuals. These orientations, following Max Weber, I should think of as orientations in terms of the ultimate "problems of meaning" which are involved in the human situation as such.

Not only must such orientations be grounded at the level of what Tillich calls "ultimate concern," but they must somehow define meaningful orientations *to* all the main areas of inevitable involvement of human beings. These may conveniently be classified as the physical world as such (one meaning of "material") including the human organism; the world of personality of the individual human being (and in some degree nonhuman living things) as an acting, evaluating sensitive (including suffering) entity; of the social world in which numbers of persons are involved in relations of mutual solidarity and/or obstructiveness, and in which they share a common fate; and, finally, the world of cultural orientations and meanings themselves, including not only the religious aspects but the fields of secular cognitive culture, of art and other forms of expressive symbolization, and of values. All these areas of human concern and of the structuring of human action and relationships are closely interdependent and in many areas interpenetrating.

> Talcott Parsons, *Social Structure and Personality.* New York: The Free Press, 1964, p. 295.

. . . our own culture is not comprehensible to us without grasping the religious elements that have gone into it. Judaeo-Christian religion, since the beginnings of Western culture, has been inextricably bound up with our major institutions—government, economy, family. It has likewise been inseparable from our thought systems—ethics, philosophy, art, science. In short, to understand what it means to be a member of our society requires some comprehension of religious faith.

To an age which is rapidly moving toward a global culture, it must be further pointed out that every great culture is bound up with its religion in just the way the West has been bound up with Judaeo-Christian thought forms. As religious illiterates we cannot possibly understand these other cultures, and it will be a tragedy if we enter the coming world dialogue of cultures without our homework done.

But more fundamental than understanding culture is the issue of becoming authentically human . . . It is hard to be a human being; there is nothing automatic about it. It involves a sense of fundamental values as a guide to responsible decision. It means finding some ground for personal existence in depth and for authentic relationships to other persons that go beyond mere externals and manipulation. And, lastly, if the Judaeo-Christian faith is right, it involves the ultimate relationship—to God himself. If this is right, nothing is more important; if it is wrong, few things can rival the significance of having worked one's way clear of it.

> John B. Magee, *Religion and Modern Man: A Study of the Religious Meaning of Being Human.* New York: Harper & Row, Publishers, 1967, p. 7.

Each person is presented with a cumulative tradition, and grows up among other persons to whom that tradition is meaningful. From it, and them, and out of the capacities of his own inner life and the circumstances of his outer life, he comes to a faith of his own. The tradition, in its tangible actualities, and his fellows, in their comparable participation, nourish his faith and give it shape. His faith, in turn, endows the concrete tradition with more than intrinsic significance, and encourages his fellows to persist in their similar involvement. His faith is new every morning. It is personal; it is no more and no less independent of his mundane environment (including the religious tradition) than is his personal life at large.

. . . All serious study of man as personal is a study of matters not directly observable. Ideas, ideals, loyalties, passions, aspirations, love, faith, despair, cannot be directly observed, but their role in human history is none the less consequential for that, nor the study of them the less legitimate. The proper study of mankind is by inference.

Procedures here are more delicate, than in an epistemology by experimental observation; but some of us, undaunted, are happy and bold to affirm that man must study man in his full humanity, and not try to circumvent this by wishing that human life were less than human.

Wilfred Cantwell Smith, *The Meaning and End of Religion*. New York: The Macmillan Company, 1962, pp. 187–88.

. . . I have suggested that the psychology of religion be defined as that branch of general psychology which attempts to understand, control, and predict human behavior—both propriate and peripheral—which is perceived as being religious by the individual, and which is susceptible to one or more of the methods of psychological science.

This definition has within it certain contemporary emphases, notably the phenomenological approach as stressed by Snygg and Combs, the cognitive emphasis as elaborated by Krech and Crutchfield, and the idiographic emphasis and motivational assertions of Gordon W. Allport.

In effect such a definition says that the psychology of religion is a branch of general psychology in the same sense in which the psychology of industry is a branch of general psychology; it is not a segment of psychiatry or psychoanalysis, though it may draw upon these and other specializations for data and hypotheses. The primary function of the psychology of religion is understanding, with prediction and control being rewards of scientific understanding. Religious behavior, like all behavior, may be either propriate* or peripheral, and both kinds are legitimate areas of study. Behavior is here considered, of course, as being much more than motor responses, and includes such things as expressed beliefs and values and verbalized thoughts . . .

Whether this definition is appropriate is as yet problematical. It is offered in a problem-centered spirit. No strictly school-centered or method-centered approach is capable of handling the complexity of religious behavior.

Research, of course, will be the final arbiter as to the future of the psychology of religion. It is hoped that the above definition, as incomplete as it may be, will lead to research programs in the psychology of religion and will perhaps serve as a stimulus to future concern for this specialized field of scientific inquiry.

Orlo Strunk, Jr., "The Present Status of the Psychology of Religion," in *Readings in the Psychology of Religion*, ed. Orlo Strunk, Jr. Nashville, Tenn.: Abingdon Press, 1959, pp. 110–11.

---

* Propriate behavior refers to that kind of behavior perceived as being personal, warm, and important by the individual, as compared to behavior perceived as being impersonal, cold, and relatively unimportant. See Allport, 1955, pp. 41–58.

INDEX

INDEX